# extraterrestrials in the hudson valley

Sightings and Experiences in New York's Hudson Valley

## Richard Moschella

BEYOND THE FRAY

Publishing

ISBN 13: 978-1-954528-67-3
Cover design: Dauntless Cover Design

Beyond The Fray Publishing, a division of Beyond The Fray, LLC, San
Diego, CA
www.beyondthefraypublishing.com

BEYOND THE FRAY

Publishing

# contents

"There are no nuts coming out of the woodwork," "We have credible people reporting incredible things." —Philip J. Imbrogno

"There's UFOs over New York, and I ain't too surprised." — John Lennon

"Instead of shunning the darkness, we can face straight into it with an open mind. When we do that, the unknown changes. Fearful things become understandable and a truth is suggested: the enigmatic presence of the human mind winks back from the dark." —Whitley Strieber

*This book would not have been possible if not for the knowledgeable and gracious individuals who gave me their time. It was an absolute honor and highlight of my life to work with these amazing people. This was true communion.*

*Whitley Streiber*
*Cheryl Costa*
*Allan B. Smith*
*Bryan Bowden*

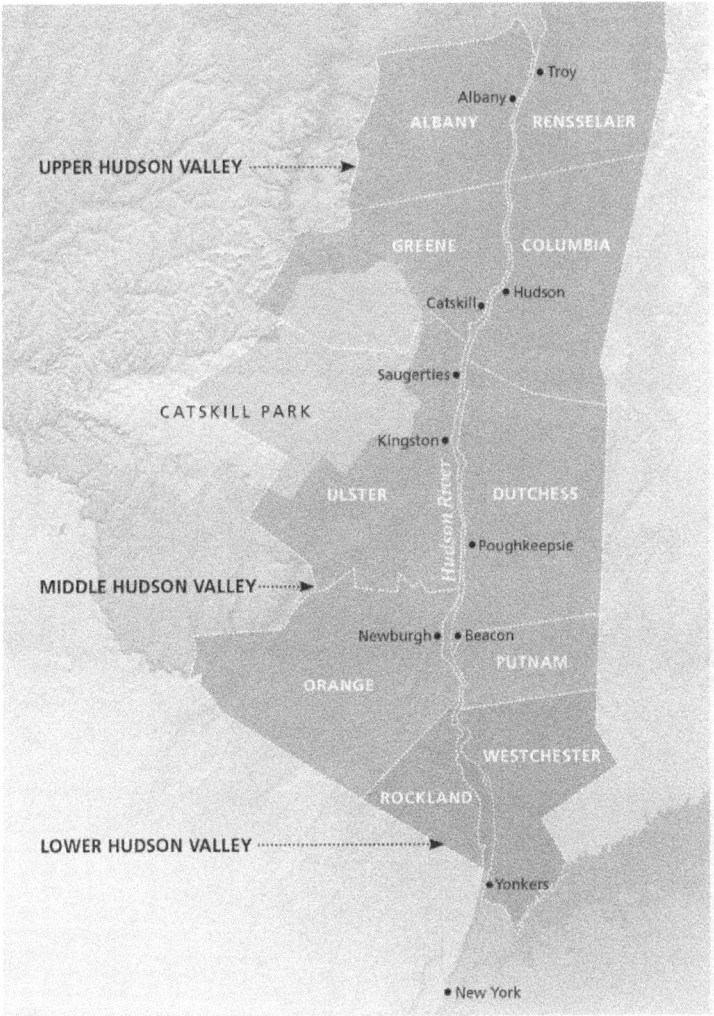

National Park Service Image

# on first experiencing the paranormal hudson valley

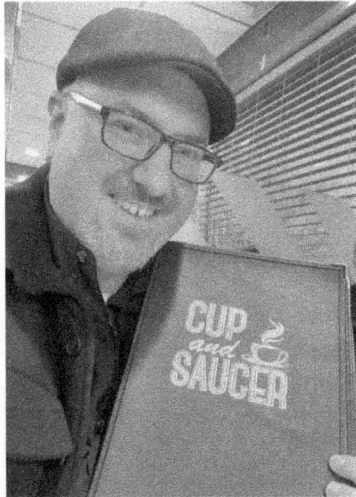

Cup and Saucer Diner, Pine Bush, New York

**MY PERSONAL INTEREST** in the paranormal events in New York's Hudson Valley began in the summer of 2019. I have always heard of strange tales coming out of this region but never had the opportunity to investigate them. On a trip to the then newly opened Pine Bush UFO and Paranormal Museum, I fully experienced the area and met some of the area experiencers of the activity. I drove through the quaint hamlet of Pine Bush and passed the farmers' fields and homes where its residents have witnessed amazing paranormal events. Sitting at the Cup and Saucer Diner in town and engaging with the locals, it seems that everyone has a story of something they witnessed that's unexplainable. I heard so many theories from underground alien bases to portals to other dimensions. I was told that visitors from other worlds are interested in the earth in this region due to its high quartz content and the possible use of it to store information or as an energy source. Some stories involve human experiments and a connection to certain blood types, while others say they are observing us as a species.

I'm a medium who researches and investigates spirit activity, so those reading this book might be wondering why I chose to write about the extraterrestrial connection to Hudson Valley. Since 2019 I have spent a lot of time at events at the Pine Bush museum and have been on many of its rural roads. I have chatted with many residents of the Hudson Valley and had the opportunity to look them in their eyes when they shared their experiences. That look was one of fright, shocked and scared by what they witnessed. I have picked up on the energy in this area and can say without a doubt that the Hudson Valley does have an interesting feel to it.

In this book I will focus on the extraterrestrial and UFO activity in this region. I hope this helps provide informative insight to the phenomena that are being reported and piques your interest to further your acknowledgment of this amazing location. New York has had other reports of UFO sightings, or what the media and government today refer to as UAP, "unidentified aerial phenomena." These reports go back to the airship sightings of the late 1800s and to the present day. We will discuss some folklore from the valley and also investigate the possible connection to the earth and stone chambers. I know without a doubt that the Hudson Valley is perhaps one of those thin spaces, a space where the veil between this world and the next is more accessible. Could these otherworldly travelers have a connection to this area as well, or could they already be here?

In the spring of 2022 I attended Ancient Aliens Live in Newark, New Jersey. The famous panel of the hit History channel series was on hand to discuss the latest findings of ancient astronaut theorists and showcase highlights from the television series. The panel featured Giorgio A. Tsoukalos, David Childress, William Henry, Nick Pope and Dr. Travis Taylor.

Before the event began, I walked around the lobby and paid a visit to the merchandise area. As I was walking up to the booth that displayed all the *Ancient Alien* shirts, books and DVDs, I noticed a father and son wearing T-shirts from the Pine Bush UFO and Paranormal Museum. As we stood in line together, I struck up a conversation and asked him what he thought about the museum and the Pine Bush, New York, area. The show was about to begin, and we were let into our seats; we noticed that we both were sitting only a row of seats away from one another. This allowed our conversation to continue until the lights went down and the *Ancient Aliens* panel took the stage. Little did I know that question would lead into about a forty-minute conversation on his experiences in the Hudson Valley and coming into direct contact with extraterrestrials. He explained to me that he feels that he has some connection to the activity and has documented his experiences with his smartphone.

Standing in the lobby of the New Jersey Performing Arts Center, I saw video after video of unexplained craft in the sky. Not only did he have video footage of the craft but on his phone he had several photos of what appeared to be extraterrestrial entities photographed in the forests of the Hudson Valley. This also was not just a onetime encounter that he had with these beings; he had seen them and documented their presence many times. He described that they had a way of blending into the environment and only being seen when they wanted to make their presence known.

He also had many videos on his phone of strange craft in the skies around Tuxedo Park, New York. The craft would make erratic movements and were definitely not a plane. Most of the videos he shared with me were taken in daylight; you could see the small metallic craft reflecting the sunlight. He was very excited by the evidence that he'd captured, and when not working, he hikes the forest trails in the area and usually observes strange activity. He feels that it's something about this area that these beings are drawn to. I even suggested that perhaps it could even be him; maybe he has a connection with the beings. I have never seen so much documented evidence over the course of time sitting on a cell phone. As he swiped through his phone's photo albums, he shared more footage and pictures. It was really remarkable to hear his story and to see the photos and videos he'd shot. I can tell you that without a doubt I believe his story and find his evidence to have been genuine.

Richard Moschella at the Ancient Aliens Live
Event, Spring 2022

I'm a huge believer of synchronicity and things happening when they are meant to happen. I was just finishing up my book *Spirit Journeys* and was thinking about embarking on a project outside of my normal wheelhouse of spirit activity. I have always been fascinated by UFOs and extraterrestrials and strongly feel that the truth is indeed out there. This was the universe's divine kick in the pants to ignite the project I had been contemplating for a few months. The first question I asked myself was, what could I bring to the topic that has not been written about before? When I investigate locations of spirit activity and use mediumship, I wondered if this could also be intertwined and implemented in areas of so-called UFO and extraterrestrial activity. Also, working with some gifted paranormal researchers, I could bring you, the reader, along on the journey of discovery.

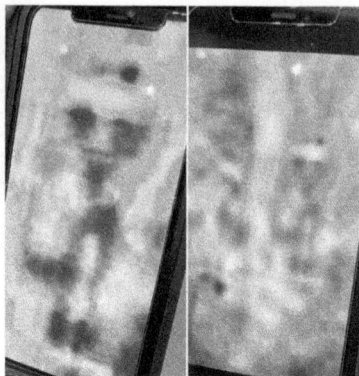

Images from the witness's phone of the
extraterrestrial entity in the forest.

Intuitively I know the Hudson Valley is an amazing place. I strongly feel it's one of those thin places around the world where the paranormal and everyday life closely coexist by an unseen veil that separates the two. From the valley's ancient inhabitants who spoke of magic happening in the neighboring mountains to the locals who reside in the valley today and share stories of their encounters with the unexplained, this area without a doubt is incredibly unique and connected to the paranormal world.

# ancient visitors

I **AM** a firm believer in the ancient astronaut theory. I believe without a doubt that ancient cultures have been influenced and gained great insight from intelligent beings who came down from the stars. Throughout Native American tribal history, stories of beings from the stars or flying machines have been noted in cave art, petroglyphs and legends carried down generation to generation. Star people legends have been recognized in the folklore and traditions of many various Native American tribes. To some, these beings are considered their ancestors, and they have great interest in our development and knowledge.

Many Native legends reference the sky and ancient interactions with those who dwell amongst it. The Pleiades actually comes up a lot among the ancient Native people. The Hopi believed that their ancestors came from the Pleiades; this place was called *Chuhukon*, or those who cling together. This can be a reference to how tightly grouped this starry cluster appears to the naked eye. The Cree speak of arriving on Earth from the stars and then becoming human beings.

When researching Lenni Lenape legends, the sky is also referenced as being a place the first people lived. In this creation story of the Lenape, you can see what I interpret as their own sky origin and possible connection to other worldly visitors.

> **Once upon a time, there was no earth, only a vast realm of water below and sky above. The first people lived above the sky, for they could not live on water. One day, the sky opened up, and through the hole fell a beautiful young woman and a tree. Two swans swam over to her, gently lifted her onto their backs, and took her to the Great Turtle. Turtle called all animals to a council, and when they gathered in a circle, he told them of the Woman Fallen from the Sky and the tree with earth on its roots.**
>
> **He commanded them to bring up the tree from the water and plant it on his great back so that the woman could live there. After two unsuccessful attempts by Otter and Beaver to retrieve the tree, Muskrat dove down and stayed down for a very long time. When he surfaced, he came up with the tree and a mouthful of earth, which he spit out onto Turtle's back. There the tree grew, bending down one of its branches to root in the earth, and from this branch sprang the first man, who together with the woman would bring forth future generations of people on Turtle Island.**
>
> **—Lenape creation story**

The Iroquois' original ancestors were "the sky people," *karionake*. The place in the sky is known as sky world; this physical place floated amongst the stars. My interpretation of reading these stories is surreal to say the least. A physical place floating among the stars seems like a ship to me. This sky world was populated and had a social order much like the Iroquois society. The sky people were greatly gifted and possessed special powers called *uki-okton* power. This power today would be described as ESP. This is another interesting quality for these sky people to have and is another trait that alien experiencers report. The beings communicate telepathically with the experiencers.

The Iroquois talk about Sky Woman, or mother goddess, who descended to earth by falling through a hole in the sky. She was a celestial being who was cast out of the heavens either for violating a taboo or through her jealous husband. Sky Woman goes by many different names in Iroquois mythology. The name "Sky Woman" itself is a title, not her name. She is a Sky Woman because she is one of the sky people, *Karionake*. Her own name is variously given as Ataensic (a Huron name probably meaning "ancient body"). In Iroquois mythology, Sky-Holder (Taronhiawagon or Tarachiawagon) is the benefactor of humans and the high god of the Haudenosaunee tribes. His position in Iroquois cosmology varies greatly from telling to telling, however. In the mythology of many communities, Sky-Holder is the grandson of Sky Woman, either the same as or equivalent to the Huron loskeha, creator of the human race.

These sky people are the creators; the stories all involve the sky and descending down to earth. So many ancient cultures look above and credit the stars and beings from above as being the spark that created life on this planet. In my lectures on this subject, I always encourage the audience to investigate the ancient claims of various cultures' encounters with visitors from the sky. You will be surprised by how many cultures have shared similar stories. You will find that these stories encompass the entire ancient globe.

In the Nazca Desert two hundred miles southeast of Lima, Peru, you can find a collection of over eight hundred long, straight white lines in seemingly random places. Etchings of animals and geometric shapes also appear at a large scale, with the biggest spanning 1,200 feet. The large scale of these markings makes them clearly visible from the air. Why would an ancient culture make these markings to be visible from above? After all, how could ancient man craft lines with this level of symmetry and precision without the ability to fly? The site is utterly amazing, especially when it is seen from the air. Could these lines have been carved into the earth to communicate with the sky people?

Machu Picchu in Peru is another location that brings the attention of ancient astronaut theorists. Ancient astronaut expert and History Channel personality Giorgio Tsoukalos questions the positioning of Machu Picchu's stones, claiming that the large rocks at the structure's base are significantly older than the smaller stones used for the upper layers. "Sometimes there are three levels to the construction—the bottom level has massive, gigantic, megalithic blocks as big as railway wagons; the middle about half a size smaller. And at the top, brick-sized stones are just thrown up there. That makes no sense," Tsoukalos explained. Tsoukalos can't imagine why an ancient civilization with limited access to technology would choose to use larger blocks when, as the upper layers of the structure prove, smaller and more movable blocks would do the job.

The ancient Pyramids of Giza, as evidence of alien involvement, line up to the exact constellation of Orion; this would involve a level of precision that would not have existed in ancient times. Also why were the ancients all looking to the stars for communication and building their structures? A bird's-eye view of the pyramids with a picture of Orion's belt transposed on top. Clearly, it is evident that the three stars in the middle of the Orion constellation, diagonally but with one star deviating, and three pyramids, also with one deviating from the diagonal, and the relative positions of stars and pyramids match each other perfectly. Even the brightness of the stars matches the size of the pyramids. Giza consists of two almost equally tall pyramids and a smaller one that is only 53% of the height of the other two. The belt of Orion consists of two almost similarly bright stars, and one with only 50% of the brightness of the other two. The smallest pyramid is the one that deviates from the diagonal, as does the dimmest star.

The Great Pyramid lines up almost exactly with the magnetic North Pole, which becomes suspicious when you consider that the ancient Egyptians had no compasses. Also, on the evening of the summer solstice, the sun sets directly between the Great Pyramid and its next-door neighbor when viewed from the Sphinx. For this to be possible, the Egyptians would need to know the date of the summer solstice, and because the length of a calendar year hadn't yet been determined, when you start to think about what this would entail, it's astounding.

Then there are the Aztecs, and the city of Teotihuacan is now best known for its legendary structures, namely the Pyramid of the Sun and the Pyramid of the Moon. These locations also show advanced mathematical principles and, just like the pyramids of Giza, correspond with space formations. Then there are the archaeological digs that happened at Teotihuacan that revealed liquid mercury, mica in the walls, and golden orbs containing unrecognizable substances. These findings are extremely bizarre and prompt inquiries about who the real builders of Teotihuacan are.

Knowing this book is about the Hudson Valley, I do not want to go too far off course, but I do want to provide you, the reader, with the ancient astronaut theory and elaborate more on the Native American belief in the sky people. This is a pattern that continues to come up when researching ancient cultures. There is a deep connection to the cosmos and the beings from above. Could the Lenni Lenape, Mohawk, Iroquois and other tribes that inhabited the Americas have had a connection to these sky people? When reading their legends of creation and stories, one could make a good argument that they did. We should continue to approach this subject matter with an open mind and not let perceived notions that have been taught cloud our judgment. When realizing and coming to the conclusion that the world and its history we have been taught might have a dramatically different history, we need to step outside of ourselves and look up to the stars and, just like our ancestors, open up for communion with the visitors; they might be more like us than we think.

Hudson Valley's Ancient Stone Chambers

# folklore of the hudson river valley and stone chambers

Henry Hudson's Strange Encounter

THE COLD ATLANTIC OCEAN slowly revealed a passage along the wooded coastline; the *Half Moon* sailed into the mouth of this large river. At its helm was Henry Hudson; he was accompanied by his crew, who had journeyed north for several days. They traded with the Native residents of this new land and searched tirelessly for a fabled northwest passage to the Orient. As the ship sailed up the river, its coastline began to narrow and offered views of what we know today to be the beautiful Hudson River Valley. Upon taking in the views of the mountains, the revelation came to Hudson that he had not found the passageway to the Orient. He ordered the ship to turn around and began to make his journey back towards the Atlantic Ocean.

As the wind caught the *Half Moon*'s sails and pushed this weathered ship back towards the awaiting ocean, the crew began to hear music coming from the wooded shoreline. The music drifted across the water and called to the crew aboard the ship. As they explored the wooded coastline and found the source of where the music was coming from, their gaze was widened by what they saw before their eyes. Hudson and his crew came face-to-face with gnome-like beings. They were described to be small in stature and had small eyes that resembled a pig's.

Hudson's mind raced; the stories the Natives had told him along his journey of metal-working gnomes in the Catskill Mountains replayed in his mind. One gnome approached Hudson and his crew and welcomed them with great cheer and invited their new guests to sit with them around a blazing fire. These little people surrounded the crew and began to dance and offered hard liquor to their new guests. As the moon moved above in the night sky, the liquor was being poured. Long into the night the crew drank and played ninepins with the gnome-like beings. Hudson, being cautious of these beings, only sipped his glass of spirits and watched as the night unfolded. The chief of the gnomes stood close to Hudson and spoke to him about many deep mysterious things.

Still having his wits about him, Hudson knew it was time to depart this strange encounter and return to the *Half Moon*. Hudson looked around for his men and could not find them anywhere. He thought to himself, *Where did my entire crew go?* As he looked towards the gnomes, he noticed large beings that had not been there when his crew arrived. Then as he looked at their clothing, he noticed that these large gnomes were in fact his crew. Something unexplained had happened and changed his men into gnomes. They were laughing and joking as they sprawled around the blazing fire. Their heads had transformed to twice their normal size, their eyes were small and piglike, and their bodies had shortened until they were only a little taller than the gnomes themselves. Hudson was alarmed and asked the chief of the gnomes for an explanation. It was, the chief explained to Hudson, the effect of the magical hard liquor the gnomes brewed. It would wear off when the liquor did. Hudson wasn't sure that he believed the chief gnome.

Afraid of what else might happen, he got his crewmen and made their way back to the ship. If they continued to linger in such company, they might not be heard from again. The severely drunken crewmen made it back to the *Half Moon*. The entire crew slept late into the morning, as if they were under the influence of a sleeping draught. When they awakened, the crewmen who had accompanied Hudson up into the Catskill Mountains, aside from ferocious headaches, were back to normal and no longer looked like the mountain gnomes.

This is a story that has been passed down of Henry

Hudson's experience with the gnomes of the Hudson River Valley. This is a tale that the local people have cherished and passed down through the generations who lived in this area of New York. The story is unsupported and was widely circulated as writers began to share stories of the area. One of these writers was Washington Irving, who included his beloved character Rip Van Winkle being lured into the Catskill Mountains to play a game of ninepins, and wakes up many years later, in perhaps the earliest story involving missing time.

The story of Hudson and crew is one that has the plot twist of an abduction story. Being lured away from one's safe place, this being the ship. Hearing music and seeing glowing fire deep in the mountain. Meeting strange small beings and being given something to drink that distorts time. Hudson is given information about deep mysterious things and then feels the need to escape from the beings. In my opinion, this is one of the earliest folktales of alien abduction in the area. I wanted to include it in the book because I truly feel that the Hudson Valley has a strong paranormal connection. The Dutch who colonized the area contributed so many tales of mysterious happenings in their valley.

## Mysterious Stone Chambers

Mysterious stone chambers can be found in the forests of the Hudson Valley. Those who have stumbled upon Putnam County's stone chambers are filled with questions of who built them, and what were they used for? Some feel that the chambers could be a northeast Stonehenge that could have a connection to ancient times. Others believe that there is no real mystery at all but rather a more explainable reason for them. They feel that these chambers were built by area settlers to be used as root cellars. They would have stored meat, vegetables and dairy products in them. As time went on, they were abandoned, and the forest began to reclaim them. This debate goes back centuries, and still no real information about who built them has emerged. Some people have even suggested that perhaps druids built the chambers about 1,500 years ago. These ancient priests, who were in tune with the natural world, have an appreciation for implementing stones and nature in their worship practices.

Researchers have pointed out that some of the chambers resemble primitive Celtic tombs and could be connected to the lunar calendar. According to researchers, many of the neolithic-like caverns are aligned with the equinox and solstice sunrises. With no artifacts or journal entries documenting the chambers' construction, this will always be a great mystery of the area. The thing people agree on is that the chambers are man-made and that the greatest number of them are found in Putnam County. Other chambers have been found throughout the Hudson Valley and into neighboring states.

## Chambers, Portals to the Beyond

Then there are the individuals who strongly believe that these stone chambers could be used as cosmic doorways for beings from other planes to enter our world. Those who investigated the chambers have mentioned high magnetic fields that can be felt around them. Also many of these chambers align with equinox and solstice sunrises. Could primitive humans build these amazing stone structures without advanced technology?

There are also many accounts of area residents seeing glowing lights around the chambers at night and some even seeing what they described to be energy beings. Could these structures have a connection to the extraterrestrial activity that is happening in the Hudson Valley? If these chambers were just root cellars for early settlers of the area, then why are some of these chambers aligned with celestial movements?

You could also wonder if these chambers could have been the site of ceremonial rituals. Native Americans of the area considered some of these stone sites to be magic and have magnetic properties. The land was sacred, as was their connection to it.

Even Dr. Hynek was interested in the stone chambers located in the Hudson Valley. While he was investigating the Hudson Valley wave, he asked a local resident to show him some chamber sites.

There is evidence that suggests the ancient Celtic religion arrived in North America and was very present in this region of the northeast thousands of years ago. Some researchers suggest that these ancient Celtic priests believed that the land possessed powerful energy. Could the Celts have traveled to this area in North America for its extraterrestrial activity and opened a doorway for communication with these other-worldly visitors? These sites could possibly predate the arrival of Columbus in the New World and put an entirely new historical narrative into play. These sites are ancient and built by a culture well versed in astronomy and stone construction. Could druid priests have used these sites to practice a religion that was so connected to the natural world and possibly ancient aliens?

When examining so many of these stone chambers, one would wonder, if they were only used as root cellars for colonial America, then why are so many of them located in the middle of nowhere? That is a very interesting fact that really makes one think about what these chambers were used for. Another fact is that stone is not ideal for the storage of crops and allows the cold to permeate and destroy what would have been kept in them. When researchers dated charcoal that was found in many of these stone chambers, the results came back with a time frame of about three thousand years ago. When learning facts like that, it's utterly amazing and mind blowing.

If these chambers were built by Celts who arrived in North America, and were constructed by druid priests, the priests were known to have a very strong connection to the high realms. The druid priests were known to be masters of magic, science and the spiritually elite in this ancient world. According to Irish legend, the druid priests were instructed by a race of godlike beings who descended from the heavens. Accounts go on to say these godlike beings arrived in airships with dark clouds around them. They had magical devices and weaponry, one being a light sword. Today, reading this account about these ancient gods from above, what would you think a light sword could be? To me, a laser beam comes to mind and its ability to cut through anything in its path. The Celtic stories of the Tuatha de Danann, also known as "tribe of the gods," states that they dwell in the otherworld but interact with humans and the human world. They are also known to have constructed burial mounds that offer passages to other worlds.

As a researcher and learning about the Tuatha de Danann, these ancient gods from above had advanced technology and imparted wisdom to the ancient world. I could only wonder if these beings are the extraterrestrials and UFOS that we experience today. If, in fact, ancient druid priests are responsible for the Hudson Valley stone chambers, could they have been instructed by these otherworldly beings? This could also bring understanding to those who have reported possible portal phenomena happening at stone chamber sites. Could this area's ancient inhabitants have used these stone chambers as observatories or interdimensional gateways to access these ancient gods from above? Perhaps, just perhaps, these ancient gods from above never left.

## Balanced Rock, North Salem, New York

Ancient astronaut theorist David Childress, author of *Technology of the Gods*, visited the North Salem site on an episode of *Ancient Aliens*. He was accompanied by British megalith expert Hugh Newman. The episode was dedicated to the possible druid connection these stones in the Hudson Valley have. Childress is convinced that it's a dolmen. A dolmen is a megalithic structure typically formed from a large horizontal stone slab resting on two or more upright slabs. They date from about 2,500 BC and were believed to have been used to commemorate the dead and were centers for various ceremonies.

Located right next to a roadway in North Salem is Balanced Rock. It's a massive stone about sixty to ninety tons that sits on smaller stones; it's a remarkable site. The geologists are saying that it's a glacial erratic and that it is the product of the glaciers leaving it behind as they retreated and that it's totally natural. How could something like this occur so naturally? The retreating glacier just dropped the gigantic boulder down on these smaller stones with such precision; in my opinion I don't believe so. This location is just a few miles south of the area that reported a tremendous number of UFO sightings.

When Childress and Newman arrived at the site, they began to examine the rock; they pointed out that it's granite. They both found that quite intriguing; when combined with the gneiss rock underneath, there is a potential piezoelectric effect. The site itself is renowned for having energies associated with it. The piezoelectric effect is when electrical energy accumulates in solid rocks and other lifeless matter. These objects can be infused with piezoelectricity and could produce strange anomalous results. Childress pointed out that because the rock is granite, it's infused with tiny quartz crystals, and it should hold some kind of energy. Then you have the area that the rock is located on; it sits right on top of a negative magnetic anomaly. This is directly under the main part of the stone. With its precise placement and alignment with this magnetic anomaly, it's harder to believe that it was just dropped by a retreating glacier.

Some also believe that a vortex is in this location, and perhaps the magnetic anomaly in this area was used to place this boulder on the site. If you place them on the right spot, when there are magnetic anomalies and telluric currents underneath—these both exist here—it's almost like a perfect storm to create a piezoelectric effect. In the episode they used a TriField magnetometer; it's a classic device to measure magnetic fluctuations, radiation and electric charge. Putting the meter on the ground under the rock, they instantly started picking up magnetic fluctuations. This reading showed that there is anomalous energy at the location. This energy at Balanced Rock was unusually high, from ten to fifty times normal. Could otherworldly travelers pick up on locations like these and use them almost like a beacon on the ground?

Richard Moschella Petroglyph Site

Some UFO researchers claim that UFOs were coming up the valley towards Balanced Rock. These UFO events were taking place only miles away from one another; some researchers point to Balanced Rock as a focal point. Theories abound of the alien craft using the rock as a vortex, portal and guiding mechanism. Researchers found that some balls of light, which seem intelligent, were moving towards these kinds of sites. This site alone could be of significance to the UFO and extraterrestrial interest in the Hudson Valley.

# Ley Lines and the Ancient Connection

Another theory on why the Hudson Valley is experiencing so much paranormal phenomena is the concept of ley lines. Simply put, ley lines, or "leys," are geographical lines that crisscross all over the globe. Similar to latitudinal and longitudinal lines, ley lines seem to provide a structure or system for many monuments and natural landforms. They supposedly carry with them rivers of "supernatural energy." At the intersection point of these lines are said to be sections of concentrated energy. Could these lines be used for extraterrestrial highways around the globe? If you're a believer in energetic vibrations, ley lines bear significance to you. People also call them Mother Earth's veins. Along the ley lines, you'll find the Great Pyramids of Giza, Chichen Itza, and Stonehenge, to name a few. These natural streams of energy run all over the world, connecting places, and are theorized to increase supernatural energy along the lines and also where they intersect.

When alien craft come to Earth, it would make sense for them to take advantage of Earth's geographic energy lines, especially if these lines have a much deeper connection with the visitors. If you are a believer of the ancient astronaut theory, perhaps these visitors have been using these ley lines since ancient times. Sites like the Great Pyramids and Stonehenge and cultures throughout the ancient world could have been taught by these visitors from above of the significance of ley lines and the mystical energy they provide. Through the ley lines, a connection is made that is global and connects everything.

John Michell in his 1967 book *The Flying Saucer Vision* supported the ancient astronaut theory of extraterrestrials assisting humanity during ancient times. The early humans worshiped these entities as gods from above; they learned from these beings great wisdom. He goes on to say that the beings left when humanity became too materialistic and technology focused. These beings from above possibly never really left us but rather gave us the tools we needed to have a connection. A connection to the earth, humanity and to the star beings.

## Airships Overhead

On August 1, 1909, the *New York Sun* newspaper reported on a mysterious ship that was seen in the skies over the Hudson Valley. The article went on to say a mysterious airship, which flew only at night, was causing considerable excitement and keeping the people of Orange County residing between Goshen and Newburgh up nights in their efforts to get a look at it. It flew very fast and was last seen traveling in the direction of Newburgh. It was described to look like a balloon with wings on each side, with a cigar-shaped car underneath it. The faint sound of a motor was distinctly heard.

Mystery airship illustrated in the *San Francisco Call*, November 1896

When it comes to aviation in 1909, it was truly in its infancy. The Wright brothers just took to the skies in 1903. The airplanes looked nothing like the one described in the report and could not fly very fast at all. At that time, the speed an airplane could go would be around forty-three miles per hour. Some of these airships were reported to fly over great distances, something early planes could not do. Some witnesses also claimed to have seen the airship's pilots and passengers looking out from the ship's windows. These sightings were happening all over the country and were being published in local newspapers. Some of the descriptions of a cigar-looking ship that was extremely shiny and had a search-light that illuminated the ground below it sound like a great description of a modern-day UFO to me.

The 1896–1897 airship wave is probably the best investigated of all historical anomalies. The files of almost 1,500 newspapers from across the United States have been combed for reports, an astonishing feat of research. As investigators, we come to the conclusion that a considerable number of sightings were misidentification of planets and stars; some were hoaxes that were intended to grab the headlines. A small number of these encounters do remain perplexing and could in fact be some of the earliest published encounters with UFOs in the United States.

John T. Daniels. First flight, 120 feet in 12 seconds, 10:35 a.m., Kitty Hawk, North Carolina, December 17, 1903

# reflections on ufo valley

INVESTIGATOR BRYAN BOWDEN recalled his memories of the Hudson Valley flap from the 1980s and its lasting impact on all who had witnessed it. I remember the Hudson Valley and what was going on there, and watching the news reports and hearing about the descriptions of the craft that were being seen. These craft were spotted flying over Route 84, in the Hudson Valley from western New York into Connecticut. People were seeing giant craft in the sky that could be compared to the size of football stadiums drifting overhead and emanating lights. These are images that eyewitnesses will never forget. Mass amounts of people observed these sightings, including law enforcement.

There is a large hospital in Westchester County, Westchester Medical. One witness driving to work at the hospital came off the Taconic-Sprain Brook Parkway, looked in front of her, and saw at least a mile-long gigantic craft hovering over the hospital. She drove towards it and got out of her vehicle and started to observe the craft above her. Other witnesses also were gathering around and were amazed by this craft, which was making no sound whatsoever. There were witnesses at the same time who observed the craft moving above a nearby reservoir and grabbing the water from it and interacting with the water. Then the craft vanished as fast as it had appeared.

Bowden went on to talk about Pine Bush, New York, and why he believes it is considered by many to be the East Coast's Roswell. They have more sightings in this town than most other towns along the east coast. They don't know exactly why, but there are a lot of theories around it. One of the theories is that the first collider test that would smash atoms together was supposed to take place in the area. Maybe the extraterrestrials have a curiosity about human progress and experiment. The area also has high intense magnetic anomalies that are off the charts, and high quartz content. Quartz can be used to store information and energy; this could also be a reason that makes this area a hotbed for sightings. Perhaps the extraterrestrials are interested in elements that are found in the earth throughout the Hudson Valley.

Then there are the reports of craft emerging out of bodies of water and coming up out of the ground, and that poses the question if there could be perhaps an underground base. This is an interesting concept because some area residents do report hearing a strong vibration coming from below the ground at times. Could these strange lights that are seen above farmers' fields and then strangely vanish by darting back into the earth with no trace have something to do with a hidden extraterrestrial base?

Dr. Hynek was an American astronomer, professor and ufologist. He is best remembered for his UFO research and his involvement with Project Blue Book from 1952 to 1969.

He also was responsible for developing the "Close Encounter" classification system. When commenting on the Hudson Valley, Hynek said that it was unusual to have such sightings in a relatively urban area. More unusual, he said, was the number of people who reported witnessing the phenomenon. "If we continue to get reports, then it could be the largest sighting ever recorded."

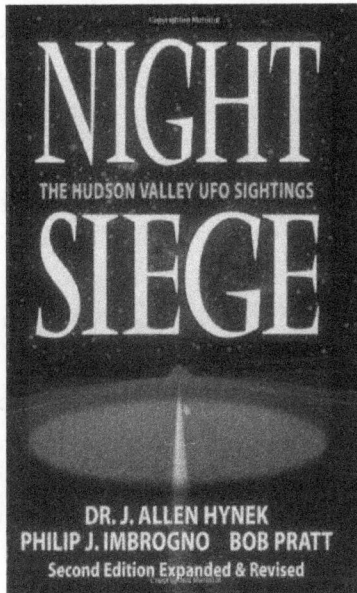

Cover of *Night Siege*

Hynek's last project before his death was a book about the Hudson Valley UFO flap entitled *Night Siege*. The book was a collaborative effort among Bob Pratt, Philip Imbrogno and Hynek. It went into great detail on data that was gathered from eyewitnesses and highlighted many different accounts from the area.

An article from the *York Times* from January 10, 1988, goes on to say, "Hundreds of northern Westchester residents, according to the authors, have seen mysterious clusters of bright lights that appear to outline giant aircraft, hovering silently a few hundred feet over their heads and then suddenly dashing away at full speed. Some even hovered over the Indian Point nuclear plant, the authors state. The authors conducted an investigation in 1983 and 1984, interviewing people in Ossining, Millwood, Peekskill, Mount Kisco, Katonah, Brewster, and towns in western Connecticut. They also staged a conference on unidentified flying objects in Brewster in 1984, at which many of the 1,500 people who attended testified on their sightings. The authors charge that military intelligence agents and National Guard officials have attempted to gloss over the reports or to try to explain them away as pranks, without considering eyewitnesses."

Many of the eyewitness accounts say they felt as if the object or whatever intelligence that was behind it was trying to communicate with them in some way. When reading accounts of contact with people involving craft or extraterrestrials, mental telepathy is connected with many. Communicating through thought is reported quite often by witnesses. They claim that the craft they were seeing would read their mind. For instance they would ask the craft to come closer, and then the craft would do so. This connected intelligence between craft and witness is observed in many reports. It is also noted in many alien abduction cases as well; the beings use a form of mental telepathy to communicate with their abductees.

There are many sightings that have happened along Interstate 84 in the Hudson Valley.

## The Reports

When it comes to the reports of extraterrestrial and UFO activity in the Hudson Valley, there are thousands of stories that have been reported by people from all walks of life. As an investigator, when you start to comb through all the reports, you notice a pattern with the people who share their personal encounters. They could be your neighbors, local officials, law enforcement and family members. They have nothing to gain by coming forward, except possibly being ostracized and called crazy. As experiencers, they need to tell their story; they need to know if anyone else has seen and gone through what they have. In a way I feel that stepping forward is lifting a huge weight off their shoulders. It also is an attempt to find a connection with other experiencers and to know that they are not alone.

The books published by author Linda Zimmermann have some of the most detailed accounts of the activity in the Hudson Valley and have been a huge help in my research for this book and should be required reading for anyone looking to further their knowledge on the valley's connection to the paranormal.

I will showcase a good number of reports in this chapter from eyewitnesses and newspapers to help provide you, the reader, with a history of this incredible area. The encounters that follow have all been documented by researchers and news media and shared by the people who have witnessed the unexplained in the valley.

A report from New Paltz, New York, from March 1960 really stood out as I began to conduct my research. The incident involved local law enforcement authorities and the capturing of a humanoid being. The report went on to say that the authorities were able to capture the being; other humanoid beings that it was with made their way back to their craft and took off. Then authorities turned the being over to the CIA, and it was taken to an undisclosed location. The report did go on to say that it died after only twenty-eight days of being in captivity. Author Jacques Vallée in his final volume of a trilogy he worked on, *Revelations: Alien Contact and Human Deception*, wrote about this incredible encounter. The story has all the makings of a Hudson Valley Roswell; the only thing it's missing is a crashed saucer. The humanoid being was captured and turned over to the government, and the close-up encounter was with a craft and its other occupants. This story, if indeed it's factual, is one of the most amazing reports from the area and world.

*Unsolved Mysteries* 1992

## New York Times, October 11, 1976

SUFFERN, N.Y. — Shaped like two enormous upside-down soup bowls, the objects hovered in the sky just over a dip in the Ramapo mountain range. The red-orange rays of the setting sun glinted from their silvery metallic bodies. One remained motionless above the horizon, while the other slipped gradually and silently from a vertical position into a horizontal one. This account of a flying-saucer sighting was not the fantasy of a science fiction writer but the coolly recollected observations of 33-year-old Suffern lawyer, Warren Berbit. Mr. Berbit, along with policemen, businessmen, schoolteachers, housewives and others, say they have seen strange objects recently in the skies over Rockland and Putnam Counties.

## "Obviously Extraterrestrial"

Dan Cetrone in the neighboring Rockland County community of Tomkins Cove, who insists that he is "no kook," says the objects "are obviously extraterrestrial and are preparing for an eventual contact here." Mr. Cetrone, publisher of the *Rockland County Almanac*, lives in a white house at the top of Buckberg Mountain Road. His terrace commands a view of the Hudson, and both he and his wife, Barbara, say they have observed several cylindrical flying objects with red, green and white flashing lights, which hover awhile, then turn sharply and disappear. The UFOs, Mr. Cetrone theorized, are probably drawn to the area by the nuclear plants. They are part of a cycle of UFO appearances that peaks every 61 months, he said. Reports of possible sightings in the county reached a peak of about 100 during a three-week period around the end of August, Since the Air Force discontinued collecting information about UFO sightings in 1969, most residents made their reports to the local police.

## Tarrytown 1976

This article from the summer of 1976 goes on to say in the middle of a decade-long string of sightings in and around Tarrytown and Sleepy Hollow, at dusk on a summer evening four residents of the south end of Tarrytown as well as multiple drivers nearby on Broadway reported seeing a large, turtle-shaped object hovering over the approach to the Tappan Zee Bridge. The object stayed in the area for five to ten minutes before ascending to the east, where it was spotted near White Plains, New York.

# Dozen report seeing UFO over Tarrytown

By BARBARA ROSS
Staff Writer

Four Tarrytown residents reported seeing an Unidentified Flying Object Wednesday night shortly before 8 p.m.

Richard E.          of 6½ Summit St. said the large greyish-colored object hovered over his neighborhood for a few minutes before heading for White Plains.

          his son; and a neighbor, Daniel Ard          and Are'saud's daughter were sitting on the porch when they spotted the UFO

Cross said at first he thought someone was flying a kite on a nearby street because the object was "hovering like a kite."

THEN, he realized it couldn't be a kite, he said, because it was "too large" and had a "very odd turtle-like shape."

"I'm not one for seeing things but I've never seen anything like that in my life,"          remarked.

He said the UFO flew higher as it moved toward White Plains.

Neither the Greenburgh nor White Plains police departments reported any other UFO sightings, although in recent weeks, a UFO has been seen several times by residents of the Carmel area.

Allan Mendry a spokesman for the

Center for UFO studies in Evanston, Ill. said he believes the Carmel UFO was not a UFO but a bright star which appeared to be changing colors because of "an unusual atmospheric disturbance."

He said it might have been due to hurricane fronts passing through the area.

According to Mendry, about two dozen reports similar to those made in Carmel came into his center this past weekend.

Mendry said he does not think the Tarrytown UFO is the same thing, however, and he's continuing an investigation. He asks anyone who saw the Tarrytown UFO to contact him in Evanston.

The UFO sighting in Tarrytown was further confirmed today by Mrs. K.

V. an   of   Fairmont St.; Elmsford.

She said she her three children, an Ossining man and a half dozen others stopped their cars on Route 9 near the Tappan Zee Bridge to watch a large "saucer shaped" object "hover" over the Finast supermarket parking lot at the corner of Routes 9 and 119 After five to 10 minutes, it "slowly ascended at an angle and headed east," she said

## The Coming of the UFOs-1982

When discussing the Hudson Valley UFO wave, researchers will all agree the wave that happened in the 1980s was a high point in the history of the area phenomena. The sighting on New Year's Eve 1982 left so many locals wondering what is flying in the skies over the valley. The sighting that night in 1982 ushered in some of the most incredible encounters with UFOs and extraterrestrials that have ever been documented.

There are accounts that go further back and into the late

1800s of area residents seeing airships that totally baffled them, because we still were not talking to the skies.

This has been one of the longest waves of UFO sightings perhaps in the history of ufology, and New York's Hudson Valley has become ground zero for extraordinary sightings and extraterrestrial contact. On New Year's Eve 1982, as people gathered in Times Square and around their television sets to usher in the New Year, something was about to take place that would shake the area residents to the core. Over the next several years, a wave of unprecedented UFO sightings would get national attention and put the Hudson Valley on the map.

A retired New York City police officer stepped out on his porch; one could imagine *Dick Clark's New Year's Eve* on the television. He walked out on his porch to begin picking up broken glass from a bottle that had fallen and broken to pieces. Just as he bent down to pick up the shards of broken glass, something caught his eye. A bright array of lights caught his attention from the treeline.

Then very slowly this large V-shaped craft started to fill the night sky overhead. He described it to be the size of a football field. It moved slowly and without a sound. It crept over his home, only a few hundred feet from the ground. When looking up at the craft, he noticed it had many lights and colors of red, green and blue that emanated from it. A bright beam of white light came down from its center, illuminating the ground below. He called out to his son to witness what was happening above their home, and they did their best to follow the craft. It slowly drifted from view till it vanished into the darkness of night.

# New York Times, March 1983

It was about 9 p.m. when Gloria Scalzo of Ossining was driving north on the Taconic State Parkway near Route 133 in the town of New Castle when she said something caught her eye. "A cluster of lights," she recalled, "almost like a town but it was in the sky." She turned off onto Underhill Road but could not get the sight out of her mind; she decided to go back on the parkway. "As soon as I got back onto the Taconic, I looked over to my left," she said, "and I saw this object with white lights, shaped like a boomerang, coming toward me, going northwest, and I said to myself, my God, that thing is huge." Slowing down, she said she watched the object for a few seconds, and then it disappeared. "All of a sudden it just reappeared over my windshield," she said, describing red, green and white lights about two feet apart in a semicircle. Then the lights started to go out "as if someone reached over and turned them out, first one, then the next, until they were all gone." Mrs. Scalzo pulled to the side of the road, turned the car off and opened the window. When she looked up, she then saw "two smaller green lights directly in front of me, about 60 feet high," which then went out. "And then I saw nothing," she said. "It just vanished."

She was not the only one to report seeing a strange object last month in the skies over Westchester, Putnam, Dutchess and Fairfield Counties. Hundreds of phone calls were made to police stations and airports on at least five separate evenings last month. Most of the reports described a large, silent, hovering V-shaped object with bright lights. Many of those witnesses experienced what is called a close encounter of the first kind, a sighting within 500 feet of an object without any interaction occurring. There are also what have been called close encounters of the second kind, where reportedly there is some sort of influence on the environment, such as interference with electronic systems. A so-called close encounter of the third kind, where occupants of the object are reported sighted, has been made famous by Steven Spielberg's motion picture of the same name.

Dr. Hynek devised the encounter-classification system and served as Mr. Spielberg's technical adviser. Today many researchers of UFO and extraterrestrials consider the film *Close Encounters of the Third Kind* to be our government's disclosure moment. Researcher Byran Bowden told me in a recent interview that it's probably as close as we'll ever get to full disclosure. Especially when you think of Hynek's involvement in the project.

## 1983 Report

It was a late March evening in 1983 that would become a huge night for sightings in Northern Westchester and Putnam. Yorktown police officer Kevin Soravilla was alone on Route 118 when he was met by a sight in the center of town that he can never forget. "It was a tremendous object, wing shaped, coming towards me. It had blinding white lights; these lights stretched a good two hundred yards," said Soravilla, now a lieutenant. Because it was only a thousand feet in the air by his estimation, he thought it was in trouble and jumped out of his cruiser. But instead of crashing, it started flashing colors of alternating green, blue and amber, making a sonic sweeping sound. "At this point the craft stopped, and this is when I kind of got a little frightened," said Soravilla. The craft pivoted like on an axis and started to move westward; it was as close an encounter as anyone would have on a night with hundreds of UFO reports from Newcastle to Danbury Connecticut, and he hadn't seen it all yet.

Not wanting to put such an anomalous report on the radio, Kevin drove back to headquarters, where the dispatcher was already overwhelmed with UFO calls. Then at about 9 p.m., when police departments in Carmel, Kent and Brewster indicated that the lights had been seen, they headed back to Yorktown. Soravilla walked out of headquarters with a dispatcher and a friend from the highway department to see if they could spot it again. Incredibly, Kevin said it started to come right over the hill right towards them tremendously fast. Remembering his training, he tried to determine a sound; it was actually dead silent.

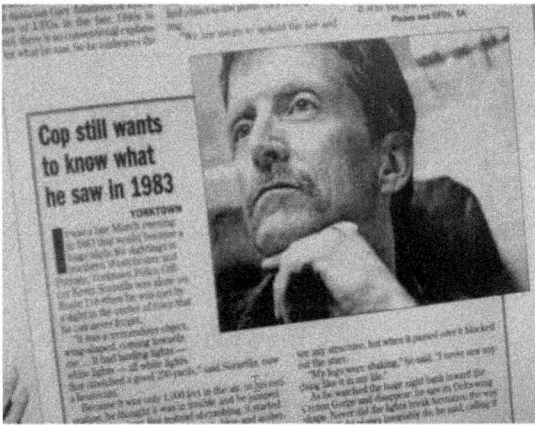

The *Journal News*, White Plains, New York,
Lt. Kevin Soravilla

Trusting his observation, he tried to determine a shape among the lights only five hundred feet above. "I didn't see any structure, but when it passed over, it blocked out the stars." Soravilla remembers that his legs were shaking, and he'd never experienced something like this in his life.

In an article from the *Yorktown Daily Voice*, Soravilla was interviewed about that night many years ago. Since that night, Soravilla has been trying to figure out what exactly it was, reading books and googling, but with no luck. The incident was profiled on an episode of *Unsolved Mysteries*, where eyewitnesses from Brewster to Chappaqua claimed to have seen something in the sky. "I was very curious," Soravilla said. "It made me apprehensive. There's no logical explanation for what that was." After the *Unsolved Mysteries* appearance, Soravilla got calls from people who said they saw something similar. "I'm not saying there were little green men piloting the thing," Soravilla said. "I just can't explain what it was."

It's the accounts like this one of Lt. Kevin Soravilla that makes the Hudson Valley wave so incredibly interesting. Not only did large numbers of people witness the activity, it was also witnessed and reported by law enforcement agencies. These are extremely credible individuals who were just as baffled as the citizens living in the towns that the activity was taking place in.

Lt. Kevin Soravilla and Mike Samuels looked
up at the sky where they saw a UFO fly over
the Yorktown Police Department. Photo
Credit: *Sam Barron*

Mike Samuels, who works for the Yorktown Highway
Department, saw the same thing that night. While the two
were at the Yorktown Police Department, they saw the object
fly directly overhead. Both said the object was one hundred
feet in width and made no noise. It was lit in red, green and
amber. In this photo from the *Yorktown Daily Voice*, Samuels
and Soravilla shared memories of their experience that left a
lasting impact on both men.

## Strange Things Are Happening

This report comes from a police officer with the Yorktown
Police Department. The officer witnessed a similar craft and
reported the same characteristics of the craft that was seen on
New Year's Eve 1982. He went on to describe his encounter
and mentioned that the craft was hovering quite low and did

not make a sound. He was able to view it for a few minutes until it made a forty-five-degree turn and disappeared over the horizon. It goes on to say that he called Stewart Air Force Base in Newburgh to see if one of its C-5 transparent planes had been in use that night. They did inform him that no aircraft was in use in the area where his sighting took place.

The craft was soon seen over the Taconic Parkway, and this time it was witnessed by dozens of witnesses. Cars stopped and watched this mysterious craft slowly hover overhead. The event caused a severe traffic backup for miles, with everyone looking up to the sky. Witnesses said that it looked like a floating city. The craft was emanating a white beam from its center and was silent. These strange encounters continued to happen and jam police phone lines with residents reporting unexplained craft in the skies.

Another encounter from Kent, New York, in 1983 had a mother and daughter driving in the area of White Pond Lake. They reported static coming over the car radio and then seeing a large boomerang-shaped craft following their car. The craft went on to put on a display of lights and started to move away from the mother and daughter over the pond. The interesting part of the story to me is the mental connection that happened between the mother and the craft. As it began to move away, she thought to herself, "Don't go," and as soon as that thought went across her mind, the craft seemed to understand what she was thinking. It stopped moving away and started to move back towards the mother and daughter in the car. Her daughter began to scream, frightened by what was happening. She noticed that when her daughter began to scream, the craft started to move away from their vehicle. This connection between experiencers and the craft is a common one when reviewing the reports. This telepathic connection is mentioned in so many of the encounters.

There is a report from October of 1983 where a craft was seen hovering above Croton Falls Reservoir. The craft was only about fifteen feet above the water and was shooting a red beam down. The same characteristics were described with this encounter as those before it. Just like those who report an intelligence and a telepathic connection with the craft, there are also many witnesses who claim the craft seem to be searching for something. Could these otherworldly visitors be trying to harness something in the earth at these locations?

## 1983—The Visitors

It was the spring of 1983 when our witness had an experience while sleeping in her bedroom. She was awakened by a bright beam that was coming through her bedroom window. The beam engulfed her entire body in bright light; she said that it gave her an uneasy feeling like it was penetrating and scanning her while she lay there in disbelief. Her encounter also describes that when the event was taking place, she could not move, her body was paralyzed. She felt that her insides were being probed as this light bathed her entire paralyzed body. The witness claims that the entire event lasted about ten minutes. As she lay there helpless, images began to flash through her mind. "Images of vibrant colors began to flash and fill my consciousness. Then this image of a being with a claylike skin tone, large head and large almond-shaped eyes appeared in my mind. His message was of assurance that no harm would come to me during this experience. It was just a test these visitors were conducting." This being went on to tell the witness that it was part of a team of explorers who are studying humans and collecting information. Then the witness passed out and fell back into a deep sleep, not waking until the morning and recalling this unbelievable and jarring encounter.

Another encounter quite similar to this one took place in the same year. The witness was lying in bed and heard a voice begin to talk in the bedroom. Frightened, she tried with no success to wake her husband, who was lying beside her. As she looked at the clock near the bed, she noticed it was 2:00 a.m. Just like the previous encounter, the visitor's message was eerily similar. "Do not be afraid; we are not here to harm you." The room was filled with very bright lights, and the encounter ended.

Many of these encounters have been documented in the area and have been reported by very credible people. Other witnesses also report to have been taken on crafts and experienced the visitors. The details of the interior of the craft and interactions with its small pilots are fascinating. From witness accounts, the interior of the ships have massive computerlike devices with lights flashing all over the place. The visitors are described to be about five feet tall with large heads, big eyes, small mouths and little ears. They assure the humans they have abducted that no harm will come to them and that they are conducting research.

## The Summer of 1984

The Hudson Valley UFO wave reached its pinnacle in the summer of 1984. There was a period from June to the end of August where a week did not go by without a cluster of UFO sightings. These sightings were witnessed by law enforcement; the officers stated "that these were definitely not planes." Neighborhoods, highways and countrysides were the locations of mass sightings. Everyone was looking up to the sky and reading the headlines that confirmed what they believed. The people of the Hudson Valley were being visited by otherworldly travelers. It became common in the newspapers, and television crews reported on the activity. Talking to a Pine Bush resident who lived through the UFO wave, they recalled that so many visitors started to flock to these small hamlets in the valley and try to witness the UFO activity, a law was put into place for a while that banned sky-watching in the Hudson Valley. People came from near and far to experience the valley and catch a glimpse of the mysterious craft.

Throughout ufology there are reported sightings over government installations and nuclear plants. It seems that these visitors are perhaps curious about the technology that we are using and possibly our capability for destroying the planet. In the Hudson Valley, Stewart Air National Guard and the Indian Point Nuclear Power Plant could be of interest to these visitors. On June 24, 1984, there were many reports from the Peekskill area reporting UFOs. Witnesses reported that the craft seemed to show interest in the Indian Point installation. A worker at the nuclear power plant told of a sighting he had. He said a UFO had hovered three hundred feet over the exhaust tower at reactor number three for a period of more than ten minutes. The craft repeated this visit another night and was seen by more workers at the power plant.

This article appeared in the *New York Times* on August 25, 1984, and really showcases how widespread the reports of the activity were.

The public hearing was plodding along routinely at the Town Hall one night last month. "All of a sudden, a cop burst in yelling: 'The UFO's here! The UFO's here!'" said Peter A. Brandenberg, a 43-year-old real-estate developer. "Everyone jumped up and jolted out. We went flying down the stairs to see this thing, just staring at it." On the night before that, William A. Pollard was driving along Interstate 84 near Brewster. "Whoa! Wait a minute here. My neighbors said they had seen something," said Mr. Pollard, 29, the manager of an automobile service center. "I said, 'Yeah, yeah, yeah.' I never believed in that stuff. But off in a field I saw this gigantic triangle with lights, about 30 feet off the ground—hovering. Then it turned off its lights and shot straight up—straight up. That's when I said, 'Whoa! Wait a minute here.'"

Throughout northern Westchester County, Dutchess and Putnam Counties and western Connecticut this summer, thousands of residents have reported strange objects in the sky—each usually in a V-shape or a circle, about the size of a football field, absolutely noiseless and outlined in brilliant lights of white, red or green.

At night, the curious sometimes crowd the Taconic Parkway, a prime site for viewing. A hot line has been set up in Westchester to field inquiries. And in shopping centers and at parties, the talk is of a secret weapon or of close encounters.

The Police Call It a Hoax.

The state police say the "object" is really five or six small planes flying in tight formation as part of a hoax. Some residents are not so sure. And others say that if that really is the case, authorities ought to put an end to it.

"If it's not a UFO," said Irene Lunn of Mahopac, "I want to know exactly what it is and what it's doing around here. And I want it stopped." Mrs. Lunn was among those who reported the most recent sighting, this past Monday night. She was coming home from the supermarket at 9 P.M. with her 5-year-old daughter, Erica, when, she said, "I saw it over a pond on a nearby farm, high enough to just clear the trees, traveling south. It wasn't an airplane, it wasn't a helicopter, it wasn't a hang glider," Mrs. Lunn went on. "There was no sound at all, you could hear the crickets." She described an object "about three-quarters the size of my house, with an L-shaped structure suspended underneath it. It actually stopped over the house," Mrs. Lunn said. "At one point, all the lights went green, then red, then they went back to a pattern of green and red and white. I felt like it was letting us know it knew we were watching it. That was scary. It went on for about 10 minutes." The state and local police are flooded with calls every time the objects are seen. Many of the sightings have been reported by police officers on patrol. One officer, according to Sgt. Kenneth V. Spiro of Troop K of the state police, which is responsible for the area in which sightings have been, followed the object.

"He tracked it to Stormville airport," the sergeant said. "It was a group of light planes. They fly in formation. The undersides and under the wings are painted black, so they can't be seen from the ground. The planes are rigged with bright lights that they can turn from one color to another. It's the lights that give the shape to the UFO." The trooper spoke to a couple of the pilots, and they're getting a big kick out of it. "There's no violation of the law here." He refused to give the name of the trooper or of the pilots the trooper spoke to. The airport, a small field in Dutchess County, was deserted the other evening. Neighbors said they had seen no activity on recent nights.

But for many people, questions remain. Some wondered how airplanes could hover over an object or how they could shoot straight up into the air. Others said that they had seen the hoaxers, but that they had also seen something different.

"I've seen those jerks five or six times," Mr. Pollard said of the pilots flying in formation. "They were nothing like what I saw the first time, nothing like it at all." Mr. Pollard said that "the first thing I saw was rigid—absolutely rigid."

FAA Seems Uninterested.

Many residents want a thorough investigation by the Federal Aviation Administration. But the agency does not seem interested.

"Why would we care about a UFO?" said Louis Achitoff, a spokesman for the eastern region of the FAA, in an interview. "If the pilot's up there with a clearance and at the right altitude, we don't care what planet he comes from." Residents were angry when told of the FAA comment. "That's horrendous," Mrs. Lunn said. "That thing's not flying over the FAA. Well, it's flying over my house and my treetops and I want to know for sure what it is."

As Low as 500 Feet.

Pressed for additional comment, Timothy L. Hartnett, the deputy director of the Eastern region of the FAA, said of the hoaxers that there were no regulations prohibiting planes from flying in formation. "They can fly as close together as they feel safe," he said. And in areas of sparse population, planes could fly as low as 500 feet, Mr. Hartnett said. In an effort to pull together information, Peter A. Gersten, a criminal lawyer who has made sightings from his Peekskill apartment, has organized a meeting for Saturday at the Henry H. Welles school in Brewster. He has invited UFO experts and local officials.

Among those attending will be Dr. J. Allen Hynek, who is a retired head of the astronomy department at Northwestern University, former associate director of the Smithsonian Astrophysical Observatory and former consultant to the Air Force on UFOs.

"You Have to Look Into It."

Dr. Hynek, the head of the Center for UFO Studies, a private group that acts as a clearinghouse for UFO reports, said, "When you have highly trained technical people, lawyers, CPAs, government people seeing what they're seeing, you have to look into it." The experts should have plenty of photographs to study at the meeting. "We're seeing quite a few UFO pictures," said Greg Dunlap, 22, the manager of CPI Photo Finish in Yorktown. "People come in and hand you the film and say: 'Be careful with these. We ran outside with our camera because something was flying over our house.' It breaks up the day for us. You get tired of seeing Hawaii."

Richard Moschella

## Underground Movement: New York Post, 1984

"Why are people seeing all these UFOs all of a sudden in the Hudson River Valley area?" The answer is simple: there seems to be some kind of underground activity in the Brewster area in the old abandoned iron mines. Some years ago the government went out of its way to purchase the land that the mines are located on, and people who live in the area, including myself, have seen military vehicles entering the dirt roads. The military vehicles never come out of the roads they enter.

Some witnesses have observed seeing "arc lights" coming up out of the ground. When the witnesses would approach where they saw the lights emerging, the activity would stop. Some accounts also state that a warm gust of air came from below the ground. Area residents also reported hearing drilling noises at night and found evidence of strange digging on their property. Could these otherworldly travelers be coming from Middle-earth? I know this sounds very J. R. R. Tolkien, but perhaps there is something going on below the surface of the Hudson Valley. Witnesses have seen light shows appear out of nowhere in farmers' fields and strange glowing lights drifting through the surrounding forests. Could the Hudson Valley be the location of an underground alien base?

## New York Times, November 1985

Well, I was a bit of a skeptic myself, until I experienced my first close encounter of the third kind. It started out innocently enough on the night of Sept. 12. My friend Mary Ann and I were driving south on the Saw Mill River Parkway, returning home from a successful shopping trip at Penney's in the Galleria. We were discussing our purchases when we noticed a row of very bright lights ahead of us in the sky. It looked like a low-flying plane coming straight at us. Right from the start, we had a hard time keeping our eyes off the lights. As we neared the Ashford Avenue exit of the parkway, we noticed that the lights did not seem to be moving. Then, they suddenly changed their formation into a cross. When we came off the parkway, the lights seemed to be only 20 or 30 feet above the rooftop of a nearby building. I quickly pulled the car over to the side of the road, and my friend stepped outside to get a better look. It was about 9:30 P.M. and a small crowd was beginning to gather as other drivers pulled over. I'm not sure if that exit was so busy that night because of people wanting to go to Dobbs Ferry or because of people wanting to get a better look at what was happening above us. We all were looking up at those lights, and they were mesmerizing. We could hear a small hum as they hovered above us.

## New York Times, September 6, 1987

While United States Air Force officials deny any experience with or interest in unidentified flying objects in the Hudson Valley area, an estimated 6,000 residents in Westchester and Putnam Counties and Connecticut have reported UFO sightings since 1983, representatives of a volunteer group of UFO enthusiasts say. The men who operate the UFO Hot Line in Peekskill say that in the last few months increasing numbers of residents have reported having contact with aliens. "There's something flying around Westchester, but it's not clear what it is," said Peter A. Gersten, a criminal lawyer and partner in a Bronx law firm, Gagliardi, Torres & Gersten. Mr. Gersten established the hot line in his home in 1984. Mr. Gersten works with Philip J. Imbrogno, a teacher and coordinator of the science curriculum for a private secondary school in White Plains that he asked not be named, to record and investigate reports of sightings. A book by Mr. Imbrogno, *Night Siege: The Hudson Valley UFO Sightings*, is to be published this fall by Ballantine Books.

The UFO Hot Line gets referrals from area police departments and from a New Haven, Conn., television station, WTNH, and receives calls from people who have seen its advertisements in local newspapers and *Pennysaver* magazine. The hot-line operators say the number of people who believe they have seen UFOs or have been contacted by them is probably higher than the number of reports they receive. The two men estimated that only 10 percent of the people who believe they have seen a UFO actually report the sightings. Mr. Imbrogno said he runs reports of UFO sightings and alien contacts through a special computer program. The computer divides the reports into three categories, those that can probably be explained, those that can possibly be explained and those that involve "high strangeness"—or cannot be easily explained. About half of the reports fall into the explainable categories and are dismissed by Mr. Imbrogno and Mr. Gersten as sightings of conventional aircraft or the planets Jupiter or Venus. The rest are investigated further. The majority of the reports are "encounters of the first kind"—a sighting within 600 feet—the two men said.

Mr. Imbrogno said that he had fully investigated 301 "high strangeness" cases since 1983 and that he believed they were authentic. Officials of the Air Force do not share the UFO investigators' view. They say they have not seen UFOs in the nearly 40 years they have been stationed in the area, initially at the County Airport in White Plains and later at Newburgh. "We've never had reports or encounters with any unknown object since 1948," said Lt. Col. John E. Perez, deputy commander for support of the New York Air National Guard's 105th Military Airlift Group, at Stewart International Airport in Newburgh.

The issue is "nothing we concern ourselves with," said Tech. Sgt. Robert I. Hicks, public-affairs technician for the airlift group. Some other military employees acknowledge the possibility of UFOs. Dr. Bruce Maccabee, an optical physicist and photographic expert for the United States Navy, viewed a videotape of a large disk-shaped object frequently reported in the Hudson Valley area. The tape was recorded in 1984 by Robert A. Pozzuoli, vice president of finance for Electronic Devices, a silicon-rectifier manufacturer in Yonkers. Mr. Pozzuoli photographed the object when it flew over his home in Brewster one night. "It appeared to be a configuration of lights on one object, based on what I saw," Dr. Maccabee said. "But I haven't had a chance to plot the lights on the object 'frame by frame,' as one would do in an analysis. I haven't seen anything like it before." Dr. Albert Hibbs, a retired physicist with the Jet Propulsion Laboratory in Pasadena, Calif., and an admitted skeptic concerning UFO reports, was shown Mr. Pozzuoli's videotape during a Home Box Office television special, *UFOs: What's Going On?* Dr. Hibbs said he couldn't explain the object he saw on the videotape but would not say extraterrestrials were involved "without a lot more data."

Because 99 percent of all sightings reported to them occur at night, Mr. Gersten and Mr. Imbrogno said, it is difficult to judge the exact shape of the objects, except by the placement of lights on them. Mr. Gersten said people in the Hudson Valley continue to report seeing a boomerang-shaped object the size of one or more football fields, an object the shape of a blimp but three times the normal size, and an elliptical object the size of a large airplane—one he has seen four times from his home in Peekskill. The UFOs are reported, variously, as silent, rotating, hovering low over the ground or in midair, moving in slow motion, or speeding away and seeming to disappear. Some reports cite a brilliance that can illuminate a backyard like the lights in Yankee Stadium. But proponents say they are less interested in UFO sightings than in reports of contact with extraterrestrial beings. Mr. Gersten said he believes the recent publication of a book by Whitley Strieber, *Communion*, and one by Budd Hopkins, *Intruders*—which give accounts of visits to Earth by extraterrestrials—have induced people to come forward and tell others about similar experiences they believe they have had.

Interviews with three women who have reported such experiences to the hot line revealed similarities in their accounts. Their three stories are similar to those of many others in the area who have reported having contact with aliens, Mr. Gersten and Mr. Imbrogno said. Many of them said they remembered communicating with aliens when they were children, experienced minutes or hours that they could not account for, believed they were being prepared to be saved when the Earth was destroyed, and described alien physical characteristics in similar ways.

Jackie Kelly, a real-estate saleswoman who lives in Cross River, said she has communicated with aliens since she was a child. "When I was ten years old, in 1954, I watched the stars through my telescope on the Knollwood Golf Course in Elmsford at night," she said. "I saw a strange, steady white glowing light in the sky. It hovered above me and I was aware of a being that did not take shape that was communicating with me and told me this was mental telepathy and not to be afraid. I said, 'Why are you here?' And they said because I would accept them."

She said the beings, whom she did not fear, visited her several more times before she became 16 years old. They came at night, she said, before she went to sleep. Years later, in 1980, she said, these beings "abducted" her from the bedroom of her house in Katonah, where she lived then, and took her aboard a spacecraft. They examined her, she said, and took her to their planet or asteroid. Another woman who said she has had contact with aliens lives in Putnam County, and asked that she not be identified by name. She has sighted UFOs three times, she said, twice above her house. On Aug. 8 she said she awoke and noted that the time was 5:05 A.M. After the passage of what seemed to be only a minute or so, she realized the clock read 6:12 A.M. She said she believes that the Earth will be destroyed and that she and her family will be saved and taken away in spaceships.

June Pope, a licensed practical nurse at a Westchester nursing home, said she saw amber globes travel past her Putnam Valley home in January and small beings float by her bedroom window a few weeks ago. She said she has had several previous encounters with aliens. "Something is coming," she said. "I think they're going to help us. They'll be here to rebuild." Mrs. Kelly's description of the beings is similar to that of Mr. Strieber in *Communion*. She said they have big heads, large almond-shaped eyes, no hair or ears, a thin and almost lipless mouth and very slim bodies. Are these women, and others who report sightings or encounters, unable to separate fact from fantasy? In interviews, eight mental-health experts in the county said they had no professional opinion on the subject, because they had virtually no patients who had discussed extraterrestrials during therapy. However, most of these mental health workers said they did not consider belief in UFOs a sign of mental illness. "I wouldn't make a case that all people who believe in it need a psychiatrist," said Dr. Jacob Harris, a psychiatrist who heads the Harris Psychiatric Counseling Group in Yorktown.

He agreed with the other experts that aliens might be part of a belief system that some people use to explain unknown aspects of their lives. "You can say that it is a way of coping with the unknown," he said. Aliens "are the fashion of the time, and the way to think about" matters that cannot be easily explained, said Dr. Simone Marshall, a psychologist-psychoanalyst at the Northern Westchester Center for Psychotherapy in Yorktown Heights. But like her colleagues, Dr. Marshall said she had not ruled out the possibility that aliens may be visiting Earth.

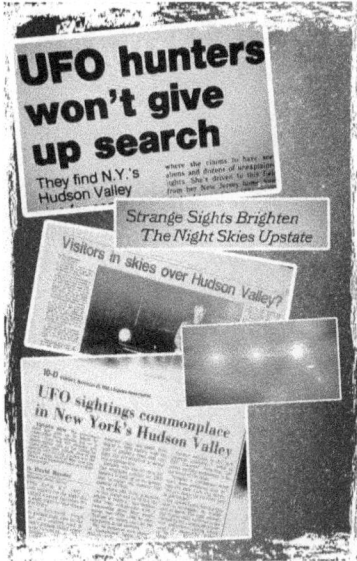

Newspaper headlines from the time period

November 1988 cover of *UFO Universe*
featuring an article on the Hudson Valley

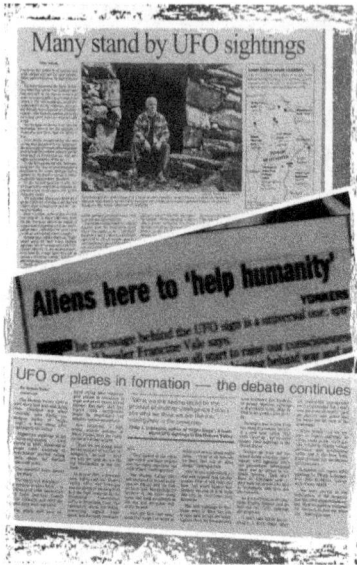

Many stand by UFO sightings

*Discover* Magazine, November 1984

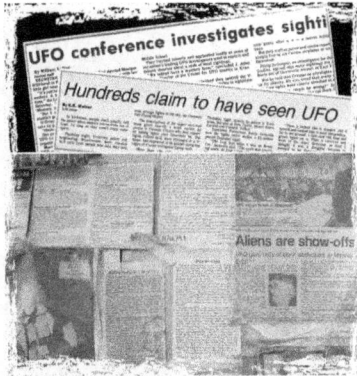

Various Newspaper Articles on Hudson Valley
UFO Sightings

MUFON *UFO Journal*, April 2013

Richard Moschella

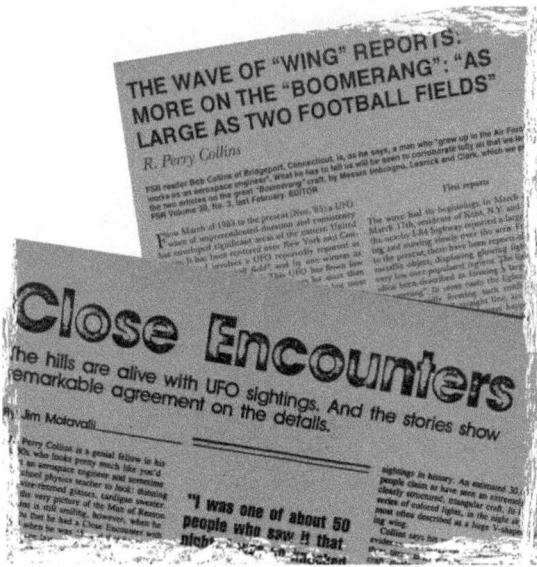

Local newspaper reports on the Hudson
Valley 1980s wave

## Coming Face-to-Face with the Unknown

Ralph C. Schubert allegedly came within 10 feet of a mysterious translucent humanoid entity behind his parents' home
in Walker Valley, New York. "At first, I thought it was a
stranger on the property playing hide-and-seek." Schubert
told the makers of *The Pine Bush Chronicles*. "It would stand
against a tree like hiding behind it. And then it would walk to
another tree. I got the sense that it was looking at me."

According to *Weird New York*, Pine Bush resident Jim
Smith is no stranger to bizarre entities. "I've seen so many of
the beings, I know how they move," Smith said. "They're
different sizes, different shapes, but when you see them... you
know they're not of this Earth." Among the beings Smith has

seen are a six-foot six-inch black-clad figure that moved horizontally through space and a headless cat with "piece of cardboard where the head should be."

UFO researcher and author Ellen Crystall is largely responsible for bringing attention to the Hudson Valley sightings. Her 1991 book *Silent Invasion* is often credited with encouraging witnesses to come forward with their stories, and opening public discourse about UFO activity in the region. Crystall first came to Pine Bush in 1980. It would be two years before the infamous wave of 1982 started. The Hudson Valley was already becoming known as a UFO hotspot. Locals directed Crystall to a field where they claimed to have witnessed activity and strange craft landing. According to Crystall, she and her companions were surrounded by at least a dozen large triangular craft. In a scene she described as "like Grand Central Station at rush hour," the brightly lit UFOs filled the sky before landing in the nearby field. The following day, Crystall returned to the site, where she discovered burned areas and deep impressions in the soil. Over the course of her years-long study of the Pine Bush sightings, Crystall allegedly saw hundreds of craft, which seemed to actively interact with witnesses, as well as extraterrestrial beings.

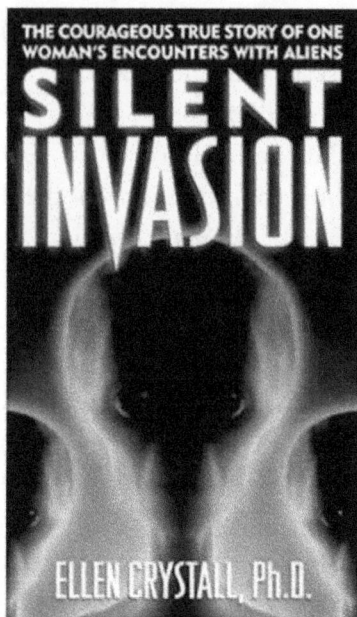

Crystall allegedly saw hundreds of craft, which
seemed to actively interact with witnesses, as
well as extraterrestrial beings.

# the people of the valley

Bryan Bowden

*"Anything is possible in relation to extraterrestrials and the paranormal."*

**BRYAN BOWDEN DESCRIBES** the Hudson Valley area as having a very strange magnetic anomaly to it. There are points here where forces are stronger than Earth's magnetic field. This energy could possibly create a vortex and work as a portal. Perhaps these craft are using these portal locations to go from point A to point B. Bryan recalled an encounter he had at a nearby lake; as it began to get dark, he started to hear tree knocks in the distance. Those familiar with Sasquatch investigations believe that the cryptid uses tree knocks to communicate and make its presence known in an area. Bryan also stated he heard what he described as rock knocks. Then out of nowhere he heard what sounded like "woop, woop, woop" sounds that came from thin air.

One of the "woop" sounds came from the other end of the lake. Whatever made this sound had to go from one location to the next in total darkness. It definitely sounded like a very big bipedal creature, and he described the ground echoing its footsteps as it walked. He checked his watch, and it was 9:15 p.m., and he decided to explore the area; that's when he noticed an object in the sky. It looked like an orange and was moving strangely in the sky. It then hovered about twenty feet over the trees that Bryan was by and then shot a beam down on him. The event ended, and he walked back to his campsite, which was no more than ten minutes away from where the encounter with the orange craft took place. His buddy who was with him asked him to check the time, and when Bryan looked at his watch, seeing that it was 11:50 p.m., he realized he'd lost about two hours.

Bryan returned home, and when he woke up the following day, he noticed strange bruises on his body and that his tongue was now blue. He could not help but wonder what had happened to him and had a feeling of dread set in. He began to spit up blue mucus into his bathroom sink, and his thoughts went immediately back to his sighting of the craft, and he wondered if he had been abducted.

Bryan believes that sound, frequency, vibration, resonance and consciousness play a very big part in paranormal encounters. He has been very successful in attracting and having events take place while implementing these sound and frequency principles. He is a devout researcher and also has met with many experiencers. Bryan has put together many meetups to bring people together who have experienced these phenomena, and let them tell their story.

He has come up with a protocol called (**CE5) active intelligent encounters,** and he describes it all being about intent. Everything in life is about intent. Bryan recalled an event that demonstrated his active intelligence encounter in Pine Bush, New York. He and his friend Al presented a CE5 experiment for attendees to experience. A (CE5) is a close encounter of the fifth kind and would be direct communication between aliens and humans. When they arrived at the site of the experiment, there were about eighty families waiting in a field for the experiment to begin.

Before the experiment began, over a hundred people were in this field, staring up at the night sky. Bryan told the crowd that he knew they'd had an exciting day in Pine Bush, but it was very important for them to clear their minds. He also told everyone to notice where the air traffic was, and it was nowhere near that section of sky. The skies were clear, and everyone settled down. Bryan began to conduct a guided meditation to focus and state the group's intentions, asking for interaction and to make their presence known.

It took about fifteen minutes; then a truly amazing thing started to happen. Bryan was sitting fairly close to his friend

Al and began to hear something very strange. He described it to be the sound of kids hooting and hollering, followed by an owl hooting into the night. Then in an instant, above their heads was an enormous craft that was in the sky. It was no more than two hundred feet up in the sky. He described it as being triangular, and in the center of the craft was a white dome. Everyone who was witnessing this was completely freaking out as the craft appeared in the sky. Then Bryan said they began to talk to the craft and establish communication; he asked if the craft could give a display of its ability. In an instant it disappeared and reappeared way out in the distance as a white dot in the sky. It went to the mountains in the distance and crisscrossed, displaying its advanced technology. It was doing insane acrobatics and turns that no plane could.

The next technique they implemented was using flashlights and lasers to signal the craft and to trigger a response. They were doing a rapid one, two, three session of blinks, and it was in no time that the craft was copying and signaling back in the same sequence. Then it vanished for a short time; that's when they asked the craft to return and be with the crowd just a little longer. The craft appeared overhead again and happily obliged the request to return.

Bryan was being interviewed by a German television show, and he said that the crew could not get out of Pine Bush fast enough. These experiments always have such unique results and show a telepathy between humans and extraterrestrials. Just following Bryan and his research, you can find all his video and photography evidence, which is truly mind-blowing. He is truly a pioneer in his techniques and approach to the subject of making contact.

He remembers a case in which he was contacted by a

woman in upstate New York; she was really beside herself because of the presence of extraterrestrials around her home. She sent a series of photos over to Bryan to get his opinion of the phenomenon. He said that just looking quickly at the photos, you really couldn't see anything; it's when he closely observed the photo that he was able to see the images she was talking about. In one photo, once he zoomed in, he was able to see a large gray extraterrestrial standing behind a tractor on the property. Some investigators feel that the area is like a Roswell or a Skinwalker Ranch, and these beings have a very deep interest in this land.

When chatting with Bryan, he offered a very interesting view of who these visitors are. He feels that there are extraterrestrials who are actually traveling here from other universes, galaxies, etc. There are also interdimensional terrestrials who come here using portals and interdimensional travel. Then there are also a variety of extraterrestrials that have traveled here and have decided to live deep within Earth. Bryan pointed out that recently a team of Chinese scientists have discovered a giant sinkhole that has an entire forest below its surface. The sinkhole is over 630 feet deep—that's deep enough to fit the St. Louis Gateway Arch. Beneath the earth's surface, ancient trees, some 131 feet tall, have been reaching out towards the filtered sunlight from the sinkhole's entrance. This discovery totally can open our minds to the possibility of beings living under the surface and in middle earth.

On a podcast called *Mysterious Circumstances*, hosted by Justin Rimmel, Bryan Bowden was the guest. The show covered many topics pertaining to the Hudson Valley and the activity that is being witnessed. Some of the reports that were talked about were physical evidence left behind from craft.

One report stated that a craft resembling an egg shape came down on this couple's farm. It landed on what appeared to be tripod-looking legs, and then a door could be seen opening. As the door opened, small beings emerged from the craft and began to walk around the craft. The family were watching this all from the front porch of their home. Their next memory of the incident is the craft moving upward in the sky and taking off. When they inspected the ground where the craft had landed, three tripod holes could be seen. Another detail that was interesting is whatever propulsion the craft was using actually left a burnt mark on the ground. He also noted that samples have been taken from the ground, and now the ground where the craft landed is radioactive. To this day nothing will grow in the field where the craft landed all those years ago.

Bryan and Al Santariga created the New York State UFO Project to be a grassroots organization with boots on the ground to examine these extraordinary claims. You could report in full confidence and have experts in the field come out and research your activity. They also hosted a meetup session where experiencers could meet up and share their stories and know that it wasn't just happening to them; in a way it became a support system for experiencers.

During one meeting that took place in the Hudson Valley, a very freaked-out woman approached Bryan and shared her story with him. This woman lives in Upstate New York and has young children and lives in a community. One day her young son came up to her with his drawings, and she noticed that the drawings were of what appeared to be reptilians. These are bipedal lizard-like beings that many associate with extraterrestrials and abduction. He was drawing these reptilians with himself and adding stars to the picture. These drawings were happening more frequently, and his mother was getting concerned. Then one day out of the blue, he came up to his mother and exclaimed, "You know you're not my real mother, but I still love you." This revelation totally shocked her, and she could not help but ask the child what he was talking about. The child began to point up to the sky and said, "My real mother is up there." At this moment the drawings came rushing into her mind of these lizard-like beings; could these be the extraterrestrials he was talking about? Could I actually not be his real mother? He just told his mother that she was a stepmother, and his real mother was reptilian. He then stated that he was reptilian and that those were his people, and he was under five years of age. Not only did he just draw the reptilians but he also drew star charts and images pertaining to the cosmos.

The child opened up more over time, and they have come to the conclusion that he is being abducted by these beings quite frequently. These hybrids used the child's mother as a surrogate for the hybridization. The mother also started doing her own research on the community that she lives in and made a startling discovery. When talking with some of her neighbors, she began to notice slits in eyes and things that did not seem right. These are like reptile eyes, and when they blink, they mysteriously vanish and become regular eyes again. She now feels that the community that she lives in is currently home to these reptilian hybrids. It's almost as if it was predestined that this area was to be their home.

In season two of the Travel Channel's *UFO Witness*, Bryan was a guest and gave his insight on the area. He went on to say that the area is very strange and has many magnetic anomalies. Recently it has been discovered that there may, in fact, be a magnetic anomaly in our solar system that almost acts as a superhighway. They may be correlated, he suggests. NASA has recently discovered a magnetic bubble in our solar system. Their true nature is yet to be discovered. Some researchers theorize they could serve as beacons and attract extraterrestrial beings. Could the visitors be using these beacons to come to this region? Bryan truly believes that something's happening here. To be able to sit down and have a conversation with a researcher of his caliber was a true honor; he knows the cases and has years of boots-on-the-ground experience.

## Whitley Strieber

*"Humanity could be clutching the frail barque of an outmoded worldview while the wind of the mind is swaying the stars into very real craft, and out of them is coming... a faint call for help from a lady in a flowered dress."*

When sitting down and thinking about this book project, I asked myself, "What can I add to the conversation of extraterrestrials in the Hudson Valley?" So many books have been written on the sightings of extraordinary craft observed in the skies over the valley. I wanted to give the experiencers not only of the craft a voice but those who have come in contact with the craft's occupants. When I think of the Hudson Valley and abduction reports, there is one name that stands out among the many experiencers. Whitley Strieber is widely known for his bestselling account of his own close encounter, *Communion: A True Story*. In the book Strieber recounts his experiences of "lost time" and terrifying flashbacks with extraterrestrials. This is one man's riveting account of his extraordinary encounters and interactions with the visitors. We also learned from Strieber how he believes they found him, where they took him, and the events that transpired while he was with them.

The publication of the book in 1987 really shed new light on the topic of alien abduction and contact. Not only was it one of the most incredible accounts of contact with extraterrestrials, but it also all happened in a cabin in upstate New York. This really was like a shock wave to the area, especially when the book became a bestseller for six months after its release in 1987. The book went on to become a film starring Christopher Walken as Strieber. It seemed that alien abduction was now being talked about in the mainstream media.

Through his many books on the subject, documentaries and podcast *Dreamland*, Strieber has been a voice for the visitors and has given humanity insight on the phenomena. When I reached out to him for an interview for this book project, he responded very quickly, and we set up a date and time to have a conversation. Being a researcher myself and a huge fan of all of Strieber's publications and appearances, I would be lying if I did not say I was a little starstruck when he answered the phone. I had so many questions that I wanted to ask Strieber, but for this project, they would be mostly about the Hudson Valley and his time there.

Strieber, an author of over forty books and countless projects, was taking the time out of his schedule to talk with me; to say I was deeply honored is an understatement. His books fueled my passion for the paranormal growing up and visiting my library. The cover of *Communion*'s image of the Visitor is seared in my memory, which I hold quite fondly amongst my earlier years researching the paranormal. My phone rang, and the voice at the other end was very familiar. I took a deep breath and centered myself. Then our conversation began.

I wanted to know what it was like living in a rural area of the Hudson Valley and having his book published and the effects it had on him and the area where he lived. In so many cases experiencers are afraid to come forward because of public ridicule and judgment. *Communion* was a bestseller for over six months in 1987, and I wanted to know how he was able to manage this new attention and the area he lived in. Strieber said he was very careful about going into public; the only people in the Hudson Valley who knew he lived there were his immediate neighbors. He recalled about six months after *Communion* came out, he was asked to give a talk at a local library, he obliged, and the event was very well received, but he remembered driving away quickly from it, to avoid people following him back to his home. This was something that the neighbors and Strieber did not want to have happen; it could have easily become a tourist attraction for people trying to observe the phenomena.

There were, however, individuals who worked at the Strieber home and had strange experiences there, and a local reputation did spread through the area of weird things happening at the location. He believes that it's a dangerous thing to step forward and share these kinds of encounters, even to this day. If someone is vulnerable in some way, coming forward with something like this could be dangerous to your welfare. When he shared with his wife the experiences that he was having, his wife, Ann, was relieved. Her reply to him was, "Thank god, I thought you were going crazy." Which was, of course, the opposite of what he thought her reaction was going to be. Her reply was comforting and accepting of all the details that he shared with her.

When thinking back on his time that he lived in the Hudson Valley, he recalls it to be a very unusual place to live. While researching the geography of the area and going into its prehistory, especially where his cabin was located, there is a huge seam of iron underground. The iron seam underground extends all the way up into Woodstock. That's where the Iron Mountain record storage facility is located, and they preserve records underground there, in case anything were to happen aboveground. I thought that might have something to do with it, but I don't really know. Just to the south of where the cabin was located, there is a road named Magnetic Mine Road. This is an area where people would witness balls of light coming up out of the ground and sky-watch into the night. The strange thing is the geology on the other side of the Hudson River is entirely different.

The valley has various stone lines that run great distances in the woods, and mysterious stone chambers. In the woods behind the cabin, these stone lines could be found. There were also ancient burial sites in the woods; children who explored the location would report seeing the spirit of a Native American in the forest. There also was a very ancient carving of a turtle that had been found there years earlier. Strieber never saw the carving but had heard about the find. There was a lot going on around the site that the cabin was on. It's such an amazing place; the ambiance of the entire area is extremely peaceful. In all places people have disagreements and fights, but it's a different kind of vibe. The Hudson Valley is a very unique and powerful place.

One question that I wanted to ask Strieber was if the visitors had any interest in Earth's resources. There have been many accounts from witnesses who claim they have seen craft near bodies of water and even have seen beings taking soil samples. Craft have left traces of their presence on the ground of farmers' fields, and there are reports of livestock being found dead. What do these beings want? He certainly believes that the visitors were under the ground near where he lived for sure. Very definitely, he found that quite remarkable. "When you get close to the phenomena, there is an occult strangeness that can be felt; honestly, it's just weird. One of my neighbors was at the cabin one morning, and we were talking about maintaining the road; it's something you have to do every few years. The night before I noticed when sitting in different places I could hear a high-pitched whine of a high-speed drill coming from below the floor. It was very weird and could make your teeth hurt; it was an extremely strange sound. We were sitting there talking about the road, and the neighbor was sitting right over where this sound was coming from. All of a sudden, a stream of blood started pulsating out of his forehead." Streiber's wife, Ann, came running out when hearing the commotion and handed the neighbor a Kleenex and helped him settle down. The neighbor never returned to the cabin after that incident.

At this point in our conversation, I wanted to ask Streiber what his thoughts were on the extraterrestrial and spirit activity. The land around his cabin seemed to have both happening at the same time. It also seems that high strangeness and weird occurrences were taking place. Taking a brief pause, he answered the question without any doubt in his voice. He believes that it's all linked, the dead, the visitors, they are all linked. It's not just ETs from another world coming down in spaceships to examine us with scientific instruments; that might be part of it. These ETs don't have a view of the living and the dead like we do; we do have souls. They are real, and we'll never figure this all out unless we figure it out in that context. To try to separate this and pretend it's comprehensible in the way we currently understand and accept the world, it will not work.

At this point in our conversation, I wanted to ask Strieber about what he thought of the wave that had occurred in the valley in the 1980s. I have chatted with so many experiencers who still remember the events like it was yesterday, and for some it was life changing. Strieber was literally interwoven into the fabric of these extraordinary events and into the history of ufology. His encounters with the visitors and high strangeness that occurred at his cabin have been chronicled in so many of his books. This was his recollection: "The wave in the Hudson Valley that transpired in the 1980s was absolutely remarkable; it was true; it happened. I knew nothing whatsoever about it till years later, and that was truly amazing. It wasn't until writing *Communion* and doing research that I discovered what was happening so close to me in the Hudson Valley, and it was shocking."

Being a reader of his books, I often wondered if perhaps it was predestined for the Striebers to purchase that cabin in the valley. In a way the cabin acted as an igniter for Strieber, not only to set him on his future course but also discover his past encounters with the visitors as well. He said that his wife, Ann, and he had many conversations about that, and they absolutely don't know. "In a way it almost had to have been intentional. I have to be honest with you, it seems almost impossible that it could have been. How could anybody have known that? But then again, maybe some did. Thinking about where the cabin was located, the thing that is so strange about it is we almost had to be right on that spot. We had to be right on the geographic plate in order for everything to happen like it did. Someone had to have guided us right to that spot."

When asked what do the visitors want with us, Strieber's reply was communion. "They want to join with us and for us to join with them. It's not a small thing; they're not here looking for cell phones, they are here looking for souls. They want us very much to be part of something larger, and it's going to be difficult for us to do this. Because a fundamental change of being needs to take place that requires shedding ego and a sense of annihilation." He has lived this and has gone through these thoughts, and it's extremely hard. They want as much of us as they can get; he thinks they fear very much that the species is just going to go extinct. "They value us; they want us to be part of a larger world. They have their own reasons for that, and it is not completely altruistic, but it is to a degree altruistic. I'm not so sure the human species is going to survive long term. We need them, and they need us."

I'm not surprised he believes that a lot of them live here. When they came to the cabin, interestingly enough, they smelled like the forest floor. It was the smell of earth that these beings had. There was a period of time when the visitors were around a lot. "It was hard, the lady visitor— it's the one pictured on the cover of the book *Communion*—wanted to share more than we wanted to share." There was forced sexual contact that was very difficult to admit to his wife. He's written about it in his books, and his wife was eventually aware of this aspect of his encounters with the visitors. His book *Supernatural* goes into great detail on these events, and I feel is required reading for anyone in the paranormal field.

Remembering when the lady visitor would come, he recalled hearing her ship come. It would arrive right over the house, and the sound of clicking could be heard. At this moment he would know it was down in the front yard, but you couldn't see anything. Then within seconds she would be in the house, you would hear her, and the cats would see her, but she was not visible.

One time Strieber's son had a friend over who stuck his tongue in an electric outlet, and he had a scar. The lady visitor went absolutely nuts because she did not like that boy in their life at all. She was very protective of the Strieber family. He recalled that all night he would have these half dreams of her peering in his face, with smoke coming out of the side of her mouth; then in the morning he would wake up and notice the boy who was staying with them had been up the entire night while his son slept very soundly in his bed. The boy's room was right across from a door; the boy reported to us that he heard tapping on the door. Then when he opened his eyes, these three snakelike fingers could be seen coming around the door frame, tapping and scratching, utterly terrifying the child. He recalls the boy asking him, "Mr. Strieber, can you please take me home now?" He never returned, and the friendship with his son ended. That was the way this visitor woman was; she was very protective.

We just accepted the fact that she was there, and she was there for years. Things would happen like one time he hired plumbers to work at the cabin. The Striebers were in the city while the work was being done. The plumbers heard stomping coming from the upstairs floor of the cabin. When hearing this and investigating it, to find no one in the cabin, they phoned the Striebers and said they could not finish the job because there was someone in the house that they couldn't see. He offered to come back and be at the cabin to let the plumbers finish the job, and the plumbers told him "they were not sure they would come back." This kind of event happened with many people they hired to work at the cabin. One crew reported seeing an alien run across the driveway, and left immediately.

The Striebers lived in that area of the Hudson Valley quite comfortably; when the lady visitor first violated him, he was terribly angry. His wife, Ann, said, "Whitley, this is the most extraordinary thing that has happened to anybody; don't live in your anger but rather live in your curiosity." At that moment he said to himself that he was going to live in his curiosity, and he would see what happens. That is what he has done since.

As my hour-long conversation with Strieber was coming to an end, I wanted to pose a question to him about disclosure and finally knowing that we are not alone. Taking another brief pause and collecting his thoughts, his comments were honest and jarring. He has the feeling that we will know two things at the same time. One, that our world is irrevocably damaged environmentally. It will not come back. Two, we will know that they are here. He thinks that these two things we will learn simultaneously, within weeks or months of each other. The reason is this: they know that we cannot bear their presence unless we have no choice. It's going to be very, very hard for us. It's always learned that when a baby is born, that is why they scream so much, a peaceful birth is very rare, and ours is not going to be a peaceful birth, it's going to be very noisy. The baby may be born alive, or it may be born dead. Think of the visitors as midwives for the birth of mankind, because that is what they are.

In closing, he believes that we all need to do the following. He thinks that first of all, we need to question ourselves. It's too early to say what planets they are from, what they are like, or even if they are from planets; we don't actually know that. We don't know exactly the connection between UFOs and close-encounter experiences and how they work. We assume that there is a connection, and he thinks there probably is. We don't know for sure how the visitors are related to us, but there is some way; those are all things we don't know. What we do know is that we have very good flexible minds, and in the end, it's going to be hard, and messy it certainly will be. We will be able to do this, or they wouldn't even be here.

## Cheryl Costa & Linda Miller Costa

"This Data Summary represents over 6000 hours of data mining, compilation and analysis spanning seven years. The project objective was simply to measure the UFO phenomena."

I was in Pine Bush, New York, for their annual UFO conference and was really impressed by one of the speakers. Cheryl Costa was at the event and was providing so much interesting data on the sightings in New York. When embarking on this book project, I knew she would be someone I would want to include and interview.

Cheryl and her wife, Linda, have an incredible way of inputting sighting data and generating very accurate reports of UFO phenomena. Cheryl Costa is a native of upstate New York. She's a two-service military veteran, USAF and USN, and a retired information systems analyst professional from the aerospace industry. During her professional career,

Cheryl was a highly visible pioneer transgender activist. Cheryl, as a journalist, wrote the wildly popular UFO column New York Skies for SyracuseNewTimes.com (2013–2019). She holds a bachelor of arts degree from the State University of New York at Empire State College in entertainment writing and production. She was awarded "Researcher of the Year, 2018" by the International UFO Congress. With such an impressive résumé of work, Cheryl's knowledge of the UFO phenomena is unparalleled.

When I interviewed Cheryl, our conversation lasted for over an hour and a half, and we could have chatted for another few hours. As she explained to me how her data system works and how it can be implemented for field researchers, I was completely blown away. Cheryl is joined by her wife, Linda Miller Costa; together they have provided so much valuable research for the field of ufology. Linda, MLS, has a BA in psychology from Case Western Reserve University and a library science master's from the University of Maryland. Head librarian Environmental Protection Agency —fifteen years. After a career in scientific research and publishing in Washington, DC, she retired from Le Moyne College Library in Syracuse, New York. She was the lead author of the *UFO Sightings Desk Reference: United States of America 2001–2015*. Their UFO statistical summary entitled THE SCALE OF THINGS UFOs in the United States 2001–2020 is incredibly eye-opening when you get to see the number of cases that are being reported.

The report goes on to say that unidentified flying object (UFO) reports are not as rare as many people think. Just because you don't hear about UFO sightings in the mainstream media doesn't mean that sightings aren't being reported. From 2001 to 2020, observers in the United States and its territories filed UFO sighting reports from 3,030 of 3,135 counties and county-like entities (96.6%). 105 counties did not file UFO sighting reports. These reports came from 20,348 of 35,879 municipalities (56.7%). In addition, these reports occurred in 18,605 of 41,692 zip Codes (44.6%), totaling 167,632 eyewitness sighting reports from people in the United States and its territories from 2001 to 2020.

What do the numbers look like on average? 167,632 UFO sighting reports in the United States averaged 8,382 per year, with 698 per month, 161 per week, and with a daily average of approximately 23 sighting reports per day. Based on the data of two national polls, 16.74% of adult Americans say they've seen a UFO. In 2020, the US Census Bureau counted 331.4 million people living in the United States, more than three-quarters (77.9%) or 258.3 million adults, eighteen years or older. This translates to approximately 43,239,420 American adults. Therefore, based on 2020 US Census data, polling data 2017 and 2019 and 167,632 national UFO sighting report totals 2001–2020, we estimate that approximately 1 in 250 adults in America who have seen a UFO reported what they observed. Of course, the question arises; they can't all be real? They most certainly are all unidentified flying objects, but they are NOT necessarily all off-world craft. Serious UFO researchers suggest that 70% of most UFO sighting reports are explainable and that the rest might be craft not from our world.

So what about the remaining 30%? Thirty percent of the United States 167,632 sighting reports would amount to about 2,515 per year and about 210 sighting reports per month for the 240 months from 2001 to 2020.

## The Very Rare Factor

There are people who seriously feel that if off-world craft are coming here, they must be exceedingly rare. So, for the sake of argument, let's assume that 99% of UFO sighting reports are all explainable. That leaves us with 1% to consider as perhaps real off-world visitors. For the United States, 1% of 167,632 reports gives us 1,676 UFO sighting reports for twenty years. 1,676 divided by the 240 months of 2001 to 2020, gives us perhaps about seven off-world craft per month visiting the United States for the 240 months of the twenty-year period.

Just the thought of seven off-world craft visiting the United States each month is truly remarkable and startling. Now keep in mind that these statistics are very much dependent on past reports and recording the sightings. If people witnessing the phenomena don't report it to a major UFO reporting service, Cheryl and Linda can't crunch the numbers. With that in mind, think of how these numbers could increase if more eyewitnesses reported their sightings. These data reports are invaluable to all researchers and give us great insight on active locations and also help predict future waves of activity.

While talking with Cheryl, she told me about an experience she recently had in Pine Bush, New York. While in town presenting at the UFO conference, she stopped at the Cup and Saucer Diner. The waitress approached the table and struck up conversation on Pine Bush being the UFO capital of New York State. Cheryl smiled at her and, with the knowledge of the data she has collected, explained to her, actually, Long Island has the most sightings.

Cheryl and Linda's *UFO Sightings Desk Reference: United States of America 2001–2015* and *2001–2020* presents data and analysis for 100,000+ sightings of unidentified flying objects reported by individuals. These are amazing reference books, and *The UFO Beat* and the New York Skies column July 2013 to June 2019 have been a necessity for my research. During our conversation, Cheryl told me how much time goes into crunching the numbers and their unique data system that keeps track of the sightings. This passion for recording the data and educating the public of what's happening in our skies is so vital for everyone in the ufology field.

Now we are armed with the numbers, and currently as I write this book in 2022, we are seeing an upswing in the reports. I do know that the activity does come in waves, and most likely in the near future this wave could end. But the important thing to remember is that nothing stops completely, and sightings will continue to happen, just not at the rate of the year 2020 or 2021. We need to keep looking up at the skies with wide eyes and an open mind.

## New York State Unidentified Flying Object Reports

In New York State, a lot of people know that the state has been a hotbed for UFO sighting reports for years. In fact, from 2001 to 2020, New York State ranked fifth nationally for UFO sighting reports. New York State civilians filed UFO sighting reports from all 62 Counties, and from 1,283 of the state's municipalities and other localities, and from 1,018 of the state's 1,792 zip codes, totaling 7,123 eyewitness UFO sighting reports from 2001 to 2020.

New York State UFO Distribution - 2001 - 2020
NUFORC & MUFON Data
Compiled by Cheryl Costa and Linda Miller Costa

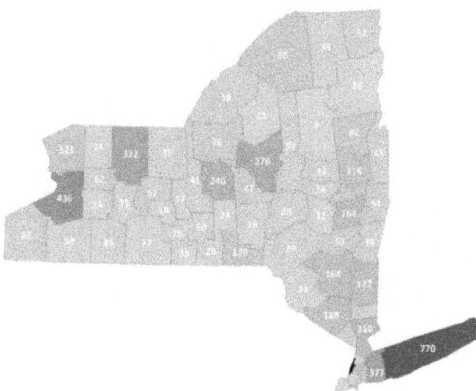

Richard Moschella

New York State - Zip Codes Reporting UFOs 2001 - 2020 - Black
NUFORC & MUFON Data
Compiled by Cheryl Costa and Linda Miller Costa

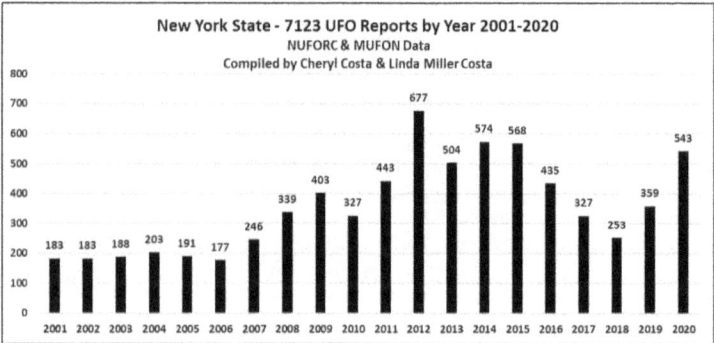

New York State - 7123 UFO Reports by Year 2001-2020
NUFORC & MUFON Data
Compiled by Cheryl Costa & Linda Miller Costa

90

# Alan B. Smith

Evidence for the Extraordinary requires
Extraordinary Enthusiasm

Alan recalled the first time he heard about the activity happening in the Hudson Valley; it was through a paranormal publication that he can still remember vividly to this day. He remembers being about fifteen years old and reading about caves in the Hudson Valley area where people had witnessed UFOs apparently coming and going. That was the first recollection he had of the area and the unexplained phenomena. That publication was in a way the spark that fueled Alan's passion for the paranormal and piqued his interest in the Hudson Valley area.

Alan has gone on to produce his own podcast entitled *Paranormal Now*. The podcast brings listeners into the conversation and challenges ideas about various paranormal topics. Alan sits down with authors and researchers and really asks the important questions and has produced quite an amazing show. He's also a filmmaker who recently released his film *Half Light*. The documentary explores what exactly is the paranormal? Is it just ghosts? What do these experiences mean? This wide-in-scope yet esoteric documentary looks at the very people who are drawn to paranormal, ufological and metaphysical subjects. Why are some of us drawn so deeply into the pursuit of high strangeness? Twelve individuals whose lives have intersected with UFOs, near-death experiences, remote viewing, psychedelic visions and more open their hearts by sharing intensely moving moments that changed their lives forever.

Working in the field, I knew that Alan was someone I would love to interview for this project. His passion goes back to childhood, very similar to my interest in the paranormal. Little did he know that publication he'd purchased all those years ago would take him on an incredible paranormal journey. I wanted to chat with him and see why he thinks the Hudson Valley is a hotbed for UFO and extraterrestrial encounters. What is drawing these craft and visitors to this area? Our conversation really captured the many different reports from the area and theories that Alan has about the activity in the Hudson Valley.

This is a highly speculative idea; he's not a scientist; however, there are some basic theories of physics and quantum physics based on magnetism. How magnetism and a magnetic field can affect the time-space continuum itself.

Antigravity craft that defy gravity, what this tells him as a researcher is that a gravitational field is one aspect perhaps of the travel that these UFOs are doing. Where are they traversing to and from, I do not know exactly. When you look at the area of Pine Bush, there are known magnetic anomalies in this area. Pine bush is nestled between a northeastern and a southeastern intense area of high magnetic anomalies. This makes Alan think if magnetism is used to effect space and time, then perhaps somehow these craft are appropriating or somehow incorporating using this magnetism. This area's magnetic anomalies perhaps help these craft traverse and assist the craft, kind of like a magnetic layup.

The craft adopt and make use of the magnetic fields and somehow assist them in their traversing between Earth and another dimension. Magnesium would be another way of trying to open up another dimension. If we look for the least fantastical reason Alan thinks of how they can appear and disappear in these areas where there are really intense magnetic anomalies, which are natural because of the minerals and rock formation elements that are in the earth, these areas are used as a tool for these craft to get that extra push.

When talking about the ancient connection between the Hudson Valley and the paranormal events that take place in it, Alan feels that it's really connected to the area's magnetic anomalies. This area in a sense is a pathway, kind of like an entryway or exit, and that's why they have been around the area for so long. Scientifically and technologically, it's the easiest way for them to manipulate reality and perhaps traverse between dimensions. When you think about the pilots now who are coming out who have witnessed these

UAPs (unidentified aerial phenomena) off aircraft carriers, they have stated the craft they were following completely disappeared in front of their eyes and from their radar screens. If craft are manipulating the dimensions of reality, then perhaps there are other beings who don't need tech to do that, and these entities are also coming into this area as well. They might have nothing to do with each other, but they have a shared usage of natural phenomena within the earth itself.

When thinking about all the reports of encounters that have been reported in the Hudson Valley, there's one that really stands out in Alan's mind. The year was 1975, and George O'Barsky was driving down a road in Hudson County, New Jersey, and saw what he reported looked like gray aliens who were collecting soil. This would be just south of what would be considered the Hudson Valley, but activity does not just stop at state lines.

Famed UFO and abduction researcher Budd Hopkins interviewed O'Barsky, and here are the details he described of the encounter. *"I would say that thing was 30 feet across, it was a big thing, and it seemed to be, I would say, maybe 6 feet high, like a pancake, and the thing landed right ahead of me."* When Hopkins was interviewed about the case, he spoke of the encounter that O'Barsky witnessed. Hopkins stated that O'Barsky described small figures who got out of the craft, who resembled kids in snowsuits. The beings were all carrying a squarish receptacle and a long spoonlike shovel. They took soil samples quite quickly and returned to the craft. O'Barsky stated that the beings moved incredibly fast. As the craft took off, he was absolutely terrified and stunned by what he had just witnessed. These are O'Barsky's own words about how the encounter affected him. ***"I was scared to death, you know, I was sweating, and I immediately made some tea, boy, after that I turned on the radio, I took two aspirins, I was scared, either I'm going crazy or there's something awfully wrong with me."***

Alan recalled watching a documentary about the case that aired at the time on A&E television, and they interviewed someone who worked at the police department at the time. Alan shared the quote that the law enforcement worker said. "No one has ever received a call reporting a UFO to a police department, it is a mind-boggling number to think so many have been reported here, but as far as I know, I don't remember anyone calling the police for these cases. We might have gotten a call or two about strange objects, but no one ever made a big deal about it, and I can't believe they were number one on that list." This is referring to the sightings, and it's entirely not true; this individual is totally wrong. There are records of phone calls and reports coming in; how does this person remember something that was clearly highly reported and witnessed and think it was not a big deal and nothing happened? Alan feels that it's a really interesting sociological observation.

George O'Barsky and Budd Hopkins

There is another case in Rockland County of a massive cigar-shaped craft that was observed on September 6, 1976. It was an event where it wasn't one person or two people, it was probably over hundred people who witnessed it. What Alan appreciates about this report, he thinks for a time there were a number of people who were convinced that cigar-shaped UFOs were kind of a new phenomenon, but they are not. They have been around into antiquity. He finds it really interesting that when we go back hundreds or thousands of years, you have descriptions of saucers, triangles and cigar-shaped craft in the skies. To this day it's fascinating that these three shapes are still being reported and are popular.

Visitor Sketch by Richard Moschella

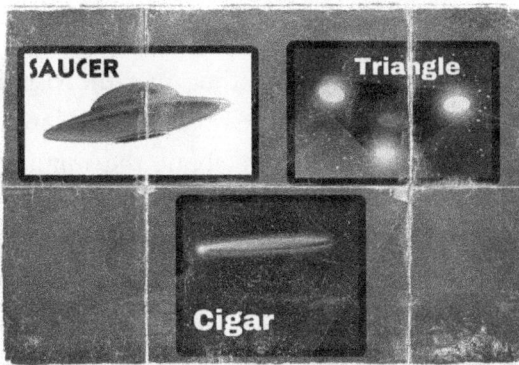

Most Popular Craft Shapes: Saucer, Triangle
and Cigar

Alan brings up an interesting observation on sightings of craft: at times craft are filmed by witnesses that are making the sounds of airplanes but not exhibiting any characteristics of a plane flying in the sky. Perhaps these craft are cloaking their presence in our skies by appearing as something we are used to seeing and hearing flying above us. With advanced technology, why wouldn't the visitors camouflage themselves in a way that would not bring attention to their presence. Alan feels that they are very aware of the technology that we have. Just think about what our satellites can do; they can zoom in thousands of miles on a dime on the ground. These craft and beings that are way more advanced can probably figure out that we are holding a camera in our hands, filming them, they have kept up with our technology, and they only show us just what they want you to see. When looking up in the night sky, it makes Alan wonder, when he sees the blinking of lights on planes in the distance, if it's truly a plane he is seeing or just perhaps it could be an alien craft.

If this is the case, our sightings statistics are way off if they do disguise themselves as planes. This is a very profound theory and to some very unsettling that the visitors could manipulate and disguise themselves and blend into our reality. When chatting with Alan about the mimicking and manipulating that the visitors can do to camouflage themselves and fit into our reality, it made me think of many abduction cases. There have been reports of the visitors taking the form of human beings and disguising their craft to look like vehicles. In the made-for-television adaptation of Budd Hopkins's book *Intruders*, I remember a scene where the abductee sees a work crew outside her home, working at night. It's then revealed through memories that they were not in fact a work crew but her alien abductors who disguised themselves as humans. This could make you look at our reality in a very new way, and the visitors could already be here.

As our conversation was coming to an end, I wanted to

touch on how the hamlet of Pine Bush, New York, has embraced its UFO and extraterrestrial history. Alan has been a guest speaker at Pine Bush UFO and Paranormal Museum and has a great affection for the UFO capital of the Hudson Valley. Alan feels that it's fantastic and quite savvy for them to embrace this history. They did not know it at the time when they started the UFO fairs, but with the growth of legitimized UFO/UAP news coverage, the public's interest in the subject matter has been piqued. The Pine Bush UFO fairs do offer fun costume contests, and the museum has special effects. The popularization of the interest in UFOs is growing exponentially, and economically it's a great move to embrace it. Why not be a center for congregating and contemplating the existence of this activity and our place in the universe? We want contact with these beings; you want to know what they know. That's what drives philosophy and speculation but also innovation. You can't study something that you don't understand by saying, "I don't understand it, so I'm not going to study it; it's probably not real"; that doesn't make sense.

For those of us who have had experiences, there's something real here. It's really healthy for Pine Bush or Roswell to cultivate a legitimized enthusiasm so it supports researchers. Because when you have central hubs like this, it gives all researchers the opportunity to all come together and share ideas, no matter if you're an amateur or seasoned researcher. The mainstream scientists up until now haven't been doing it, and it's really been up to the amateurs.

Historically there have been amateur astronomers, archaeologists or even people who are not nearly amateurs like Marie Curie, extremely smart and educated, but her interests in radioactivity and research into treatments for cancer were considered novel for her time, and she was kind of amateurish considering she kept a bottle of polonium on her nightstand. But if you could have someone who was "crazy enough" to do something that no one else would do or believe in, you wouldn't be breaking down new barriers for science.

The Pine Bush UFO and Paranormal Museum

Alan feels that these kinds of gatherings, whether it's an event like the UFO conference or going to the Pine Bush Museum to listen to a featured speaker, it's all a spearhead for legitimization. It's all pushing the momentum and subject matter forward. The sociology side of it is, humans need to wonder, we need speculation, we need new myths too. It's highly healthy, so whether someone says they saw bigfoot and it gets a little bit of coverage from those mini stories, whether it's a real bigfoot or not, it fills that void that we sometimes have that mythology has always served. Religion is different than mythology, though Alan feels that religion is essentially mythology, but mythology is storytelling. We can't always have the same stories told over and over again. We need our own mini myths, and in our current times, to break up the monotony and make us wonder about what else is out there.

# abduction

Richard Moschella Sketch of Alien Abduction

IN THE *MUFON JOURNAL* #156 dated February 1981, an article was featured that was written by Budd Hopkins. Hopkins spent his entire life researching the abduction phenomena. His books *Missing Time* and *Intruders* were groundbreaking and really gave a voice to abductees. The article shared the story of a sixty-one-year-old woman who he named her, was outside

was a retired schoolteacher. At the time she was only nine years old and was playing outside her home near Spring Valley, New York. When telling her story about the encounter, she used the words "strange peculiar experience."

"Ellen Sutter," as Hopkins named her, was outside playing by a very large oak tree. Little did she know that she was about to witness something otherworldly. It was an overcast summer afternoon, and the sun was waning down in the sky. That is when she said she witnessed a blinding flash of light, like sunlight on metal. Looking above her, she noticed something over the tall trees. The object was huge and shaped like a dirigible (airship). The object had many portholes and a very peculiar light emanating from it. As she was watching it, she said it felt like time stood still. This is very common with abduction cases, manipulation of time and space. She also felt like she was rooted to the spot she was standing in and could not move. Another aspect of abduction cases is paralysis. The next part of this story is truly remarkable; she noticed several beings come out of the craft and float in midair.

The beings were described as wearing diving suits with a head shape on top and a very distorted, short-looking body. She said the figures were back inside their craft as quick as snapping your fingers. Ellen had no idea how long the entire event lasted, but when she finally returned home, her mother was extremely upset. Her mother scolded her for being gone for so long. This is another part of the story that many abductees report, missing time. An event that felt like it lasted only minutes could in fact be hours. She never told her mother about the incident; she knew it would sound crazy. She also felt that she needed to keep the incident a secret.

In the days and months after the incident, Ellen was very much afraid of it happening again. She developed a fear of being alone and never felt safe. This was followed by a fear of getting sick and needing to go to a hospital. This fear also manifested in night terrors. Many abductees report the after-effects of an abduction. When the subconscious mind is accessible during sleep, the blocks that were put in place go down. This could result in suppressed memories and traumas coming to the surface.

Another aspect of the case that is interesting is that this was 1929 America. This was many years before Kenneth Arnold's sighting and giving the objects he witnessed the name flying saucers and the infamous UFO crash in Roswell, New Mexico. UFO hysteria had not yet exploded in newspaper headlines and gripped the public's imaginations.

After reading this encounter, I wondered if Ellen had any more encounters with these craft and beings. Her story has every facet of a typical abduction encounter. Abductees are usually plagued by these encounters throughout their lives. Abductions are also reported in family bloodlines. I wish we could have had the time to sit down with Ellen and explore if she had any more encounters throughout her life. I would almost bet that she probably did. The account she left is extremely vivid. That afternoon in Spring Valley, New York, in 1929 would be a day Ellen would never forget, and the encounter is still being talked about all these years later.

The residents of the valley have reported many abduction encounters and also witnessed alien beings in the surrounding countryside. One report that I read was reported by a motorist who witnessed the typical gray aliens in the woods as she was driving along a wooded road at night.

Her headlights illuminated them and caused such fright and panic she drove off as fast as she could. Other reports by abductees is that it seems that time itself is stopped, birds stop chirping, and all noises cease. Then after the abduction takes place, it seems that only a few minutes have gone by, but in fact it could be hours later. These beings seem to have the technology to manipulate time itself.

Some abductees also report that the beings are also able to cloak themselves and become transparent. In some cases the witnesses claim to have felt a very strong presence of not being alone, being watched, and hearing the beings in their home. This also could sound like spirit activity and hearing phantom footsteps and noises. Some feel that spirit activity and extraterrestrial beings are very closely related and that our human minds cannot comprehend how they are connected to one another. This can be further explored in the writings of Whitley Strieber in his books *A New World*, *The Key* and *Communion*.

There is another aspect of alien abduction that is right out of a horror film: the idea of being taken against one's will and having a series of horrendous medical tests performed is absolutely terrifying. These reports mention that the abductees felt immense pain and felt violated by their alien captors. These abduction reports also reveal some motive behind the abduction as a possible alien cloning experiment and perhaps genetically blending human and alien DNA. This would then suggest that the aliens are working on a hybrid species.

I was reading an article that was published on May 25, 2019, by NBC News; it was written by Seth Shostak. It offered a much newer perspective on the reason for the aliens creating a hybrid race. An instructor at the University of Oxford in England believes the abductions are real. Young-hae Chi, who teaches Korean at the university, also claims to know what the aliens have in mind. In lectures given at the university, he says they're creating alien-human hybrids as a hedge against climate change. To support his unorthodox theory, Chi notes that for several decades the number of reported alien abductions has risen. He bases this statement on the work of David Jacobs, a retired Temple University historian who has published several books on ufology. Jacobs has interviewed more than a thousand people who claim to have been abducted, using hypnotic regression that apparently allows them to recall their unearthly encounters with aliens. (Mind you, this too is controversial, and Jacobs himself admits that people should be skeptical of these recollections.)

Chi takes the claims at face value and links the growing number of abductees cataloged by Jacobs to the increase in atmospheric greenhouse gasses. He doesn't imply a cause and effect: the abduction experiment is not responsible for global warming. Rather, it's a reaction to it. The extraterrestrials are producing hybrids who can better withstand the rigors of a toastier planet. By producing a new model of *Homo sapiens*, this project would eliminate the need for difficult climate accords or elaborate geoengineering projects. It would also help the aliens themselves — who are said to be living among us — by preserving the part of their DNA that's carried by the temperature-tolerant hybrids.

In an interview, David Jacobs recalled when his friend and researcher Budd Hopkins reached out to him about an astounding story that he wanted to share with him. It involved a woman being taken on board a craft and was subjected to various procedures. The beings took her into another room, and that's when the beings presented her with a very strange-looking baby. David Jacobs thought to himself, *That's very odd, the word baby and UFO have never been said in the same sentence before,* as far as he could recall. Hopkins explained that the beings wanted the woman to hold the baby and then to feed the baby. This was all inconceivable to Jacobs because she was not lactating or pregnant. The beings were forcing the woman to do this and pushed the baby to the woman's breast. Jacobs thought to himself, *We will never be able to understand how these beings think. Because they value form over function. They put the baby to this woman's breast, which is the form of feeding, but because she's not lactating, there is no function.* They then later learned that the women was in fact lactating; the beings stimulated lactation.

They also wanted to see the way a human mother would hold the child. This also reminds me of the skin-to-skin method when a baby is born; it's important that skin-to-skin contact is made with the newborn baby. The benefits can range from calming and relaxing both mother and baby. It also helps regulate the baby's heart rate and breathing, helping them to better adapt to life outside the womb. This contact also stimulates digestion and an interest in feeding. Other benefits are oxygen, temperature and growth, could this be why the beings want these alien hybrids held by humans? Maybe it imparts just enough human contact and emotion to the hybrid child and supports its health. The visitors might want to observe how a mother interacts with the child.

## The Blood Connection

There is a biological and reproductive interest between the aliens and humans. An article by the staff at Gaia was extremely insightful and spoke of the possible blood connection with abductees. Some investigators and experiencers believe that the aliens might seek certain blood types among humans on Earth, and this is why certain humans are abducted while others are not.

In the continued search for the origin of mankind and our first ancestors, incomplete data leaves gaps in the path tracing our genetic lineage back through history. According to the evolutionists, our ancestry can be traced back through mutations in our DNA caused by our environmental surroundings and adaptation to changes for survival—a gradual improvement over millions of years from ape to *Homo sapiens*. According to creationists, some powerful, all-knowing, outside being or force invented us instantaneously and directed our lives—we are as we were at inception, from the first human being up till now. But what if the answer is a combination of both?

Meet the rhesus monkey. Though science today has proven that the human genome shares approximately 97% of the same DNA sequence with primates, the rhesus monkey is unique in its timing and fame in the modern medical world.

- In 1901, Austrian-born Dr. Karl Landsteiner used a mix of rhesus monkey and rabbit blood to determine agglutination, a clumping response in certain combinations of blood that led to the discovery of blood types A, B, O and AB and explained previous violent reactions and sometimes death from blood transfusions. This led to blood typing and higher success rates in transfusions.

- Twenty-nine years later, in 1930, furthering research on blood; Landsteiner repeated the procedure using human and rhesus monkey blood. There he found a common factor between the rhesus monkey blood and human blood in its clumping response, dubbing the factor as Rh positive—having the same factor as the rhesus monkey.

- Approximately 85% of the human population is Rh positive, where blood cells contain the D antigen, as it was called, a substance on the surface of the red blood cell that triggers antibodies. Those without the Rh factor or D antigen, called Rh negative, comprise only 15% of the population.

These discoveries were just the tip of the iceberg in blood type and health research; however, it revealed an anomaly—a mysterious effect of Rh negative that naturally occurs only in humans. When the mother is Rh negative and the father is Rh positive, the resulting baby will most likely be Rh positive —the consistently most dominant factor. The Rh-positive baby could then trigger the antibodies of its Rh-negative mother, and her body would attack the "foreign" blood cells of the baby. Rh negative does not "receive" Rh positive. The "positive" is an additional trait to the blood shared by other species on Earth. Rh negative means that this trait is not present, and in the case of Rh-negative pregnant mothers, the Rh-positive trait is not accepted by her blood or body, and like an impurity, it is fought off by the immune system. In addition, because Rh positive shares the trait similarity with other species, specifically apes, the Rh-positive bloodline can be mapped through time and evolution. Rh negative cannot. It has no similarities or earthly trace. So where did Rh negative come from?

Since the discovery of blood types over a hundred years ago, little else has been identified by science as to how our blood types originated and why they exist at all. However, in putting together the history of evidence and modern science, theorists believe the Rh-negative blood type points to alien ancestors and the merging of two distinct DNAs. Believers hypothesize that aliens continue to experiment and improve upon their design by abducting humans. Others say they need our organs and blood for transfusions, transplants or cloning an interstellar colonization. The singularity of Rh negative, the elements in the details of recorded history and legend, the compiling accounts, and a revealing component —the highest number of alien abductees are Rh negative— produces compelling evidence linking the alien abductions to not only their very real existence but also their extensive and ongoing contact with Earth.

The reason for abductions remains a mystery, and the possibilities for why they visit Earth or whom they choose to abduct appear to go beyond some simple family reunion or friendly deep-space neighborly contact. However, as we ourselves continue our own genetic research and push the limits on cloning and DNA splicing, and uncover more evidence connecting the microscopic building blocks to all life and the universe, the potential of biological similarities with beings from another world doesn't seem so impossible.

If extraterrestrials continue to visit and share a blood trait with Rh negatives, preferring to abduct them over others, are RH negatives safe? There currently is no definitive way that has been presented or shared with the public to prevent alien abductions. Suggestions from believers and abductees seem to point narrowly to wearing protective gear that blocks mind control and good old-fashioned mental and physical resistance.

However, there are a consistent number of common traits that show up for Rh negatives:

- Extra vertebrae
- Higher-than-average IQ
- More sensitive vision and other senses
- Lower body temperature
- Higher blood pressure
- Increased occurrence of psychic/intuitive abilities
- Predominantly blue, green, or hazel eyes
- Red or reddish hair
- Increased sensitivity to heat and sunlight
- Cannot be cloned (on Earth)
- Higher rates of alien abduction and other unexplained phenomena

Armed with a better understanding of your blood type and possibly the revelation of shared characteristics and personal experiences, you can be better prepared to face an alien abduction or find more answers in the collective of abductees.

In either case, the imperative seems to be don't wait to find out, and search deeply for answers.

Maybe there will never be a solid conclusion or answer to why we have different blood types or where they originated, or why extraterrestrials continue to visit Earth. What we do know is that the stories that have pervaded our existence, from the beginning of our perceived time to the present, have left room in our rational minds for the possibility of "others" and their significance in our own development. Quite possibly our own mysterious biological natures are linked to theirs and may be tied closer to some human beings and ancestries than others.

Perhaps the number of reported alien abductions being those with Rh-negative blood is random, or perhaps it is the indicator of an unbreakable relationship between man and the "Gods." We may never know absolutely. In the meantime, Rh negatives, especially the universal donor, O-negative, can consider that their blood is rare and valuable and could have the potential to save anyone on Earth and conceivably others throughout the universe.

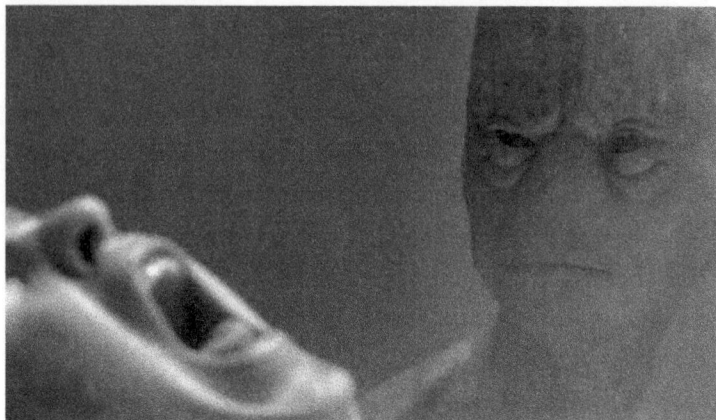

*Fire in the Sky* Film 1993 Paramount Pictures

The owl has held a place of reverence and mystique throughout history. And as strange as this might seem, owls are also showing up in conjunction with the UFO experience. Many experiencers of the abduction phenomenon have reported seeing owls at or around the time of their abduction experience. Could the extraterrestrials be using the imagery of an owl to cloak themselves when interacting with humans? Is it possible that they could be influencing the people experiencing the phenomenon to see something other than an alien presence? This could be a tactic to keep the abductee calm and not suspect something sinister is happening. This is a common "screen memory" that is remembered after an experience; abductees have reported seeing owls that were as big as two to three feet tall.

Screen Memory: Owls and Extraterrestrials

In an interview with the author of possibly the most famous alien abduction story ever, *Communion*, Whitley Strieber explained that long before he started having abduction experiences, "There was a white owl that used to stand in our backyard and watch the windows of my bedroom when I was a child. It made my folks nervous. This was during the time that they started nailing the screens shut." This cloaking also can be looked at as a way to make the encounter less traumatic to the experiencer and help blend into memory.

115

I have had an interesting experience with an owl that I never shared with anyone; it was during a snowstorm at my home in Northern New Jersey. I woke up and walked to my kitchen to peer out the window and see how the conditions outside looked. I would make the judgment call if I was going to attempt to drive into work or to call out. Something in my yard caught my eye; it was perched on a branch in the woods about fifty feet from my window. I thought to myself, "Could that be an owl?" It was white, and now looking at owl species in New Jersey, I would say it was a snowy owl. We locked eyes for a few seconds, and then it flew towards the kitchen window and vanished over the house. I called out of work and went back to sleep; nothing profound happened or was experienced that I could recall. While researching this book and learning about the owl and extraterrestrial connection, I wonder if it was just an owl in my yard that night or perhaps something else.

It's incidents like this one I have described that so many abduction experiencers report; there are also reports of telepathy happening between the aliens and the humans. I recently read a book by Mike Clelland entitled *The Messengers: Owls, Synchronicity and the UFO Abductee.* The book is an in-depth study on owls and their deep connection to the paranormal world; for Clelland it all began with owls circling overhead for an entire hour during a 2006 camping trip. He was familiar with the UFO-owl connection and intuitively felt something mystical was happening, even perhaps otherworldly. Clelland then connects owl experiences with his own alien abductions and also shares many encounters with individuals who shared their experiences with him.

The book was extremely jarring and also prompted me to

rethink and try to remember that winter night in my kitchen. These people are having extraordinary experiences with nonhuman intelligence. What follows are the classic abduction reports of missing time, telepathy and paralysis. In an interview Clelland does mention that not all owl encounters are them doing the bidding for aliens. "I don't think the UFO's occupants are pushing a little button and saying 'calling all owls,' meet us at this spot to give this person a psychic experience." He thinks it's happening in a much more mystical and overlapping way than that. One abductee remembers that he saw owls constantly around his home over a period of time, and once he began the hypnosis process, startling abduction experiences were revealed.

Richard Dolan said, in the introduction to the book *The Messengers*, something very odd is going on in our world; it is not simply the manifestation into our physical reality of things that Western culture merely considers symbolic or archetypal. It is also that these manifestations appear in a bizarrely synchronistic manner. It is as if someone or some intelligence is pulling the strings of our reality and doing so in order to tell us something. To teach us.

Richard Moschella

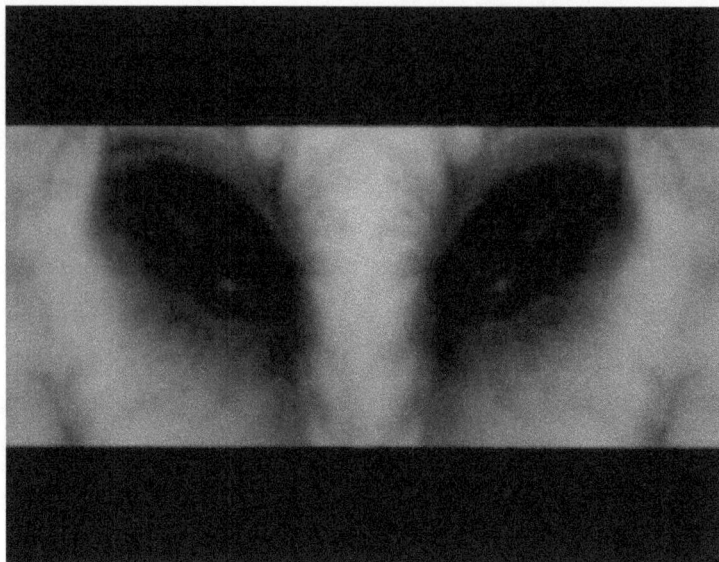

*The Fourth Kind*, 2009

# budd hopkins

"An Extraordinary Phenomenon demands an extraordinary investigation."

**THE FIRST PERSON** to ever really collect and publish such stories in quantity on alien abduction was Budd

Hopkins. Hopkins is widely credited with having begun the alien-abduction movement, a subgenre of UFO studies. His books—*Intruders: The Incredible Visitations at Copley Woods*; *Witnessed: The True Story of the Brooklyn Bridge UFO Abductions*; *Missing Time*; *Sight Unseen: Science, UFO Invisibility, Transgenic Beings*; and *Art, Life and UFOs: A Memoir*—have been highly regarded among researchers in the field. Three of Hopkins's books went on to be *New York Times* bestsellers and seminal books on abduction phenomenon. He appeared on hundreds of national television and radio programs and was even enlisted by Steven Spielberg to be a spokesperson for his miniseries *Taken*. Hopkins was also a very gifted and renowned artist. His abstract expressionist paintings and sculptures have been featured in countless fine art museums. Sadly, he passed away on August 21, 2011, from complications from cancer.

His work is still relevant today and being studied by new researchers in the field; his interviews with abductees and experiencers have given a voice to the phenomenon and credibility. I was first introduced to Hopkins while watching a television show that featured paranormal topics in the 1990s called *Sightings*. I later went on to read all of his books on the subject of abduction, but it was the made-for-television miniseries from 1992 that was based on his book *Intruders* that really sparked my interest and fueled my curiosity on the subject. The film featured fictionalized characters based on the works of Hopkins and John E. Mack. The scenes and message of the movie were very real and at times extremely unsettling. The film made a lasting impact on me and fueled my passion for the paranormal.

Hopkins also worked with Whitley Strieber and the

Harvard psychiatrist John Mack; they have both credited him with having ignited their interest in the field. In Whitley Strieber's book *Communion*, Hopkins is one of the researchers who assists in the hypnosis therapy that helped reveal the abduction claims that Strieber went through. Hopkins also interviewed many experiencers in the Hudson Valley and needs to be included in the history of the phenomena in this area.

It's people like Hopkins, who devoted the rest of his life to the subject of alien abduction, who really need to be commended and remembered. He was always quick to point out that he had never been abducted himself but did in fact have an experience with a UFO on Cape Cod in 1964. This prompted him to begin gathering stories of adventurers who encountered unexplained craft and alien beings. Some of these interviews with experiencers would then reveal an aspect of the UFO experience known as alien abduction and involve involuntary and unpleasant procedures being done to them by their alien abductors.

Hopkins could not help but notice the similarity in the encounters that were reported. The lonely road, the dark of night, the burst of light, the sudden passage through the air and into a waiting craft, and above all, the sense of time that could not be accounted for. This would be known as missing time and is a major factor in the abduction experience. The beings were described as being short with bug eyes, thin lips and gray skin. The most popular image of extraterrestrials, today we call them the grays.

When abducted men would have sperm removed and women would claim to have their eggs harvested by the beings, one of Hopkins theories was that the "visitors" were practicing a form of extraterrestrial eugenics and aiming to shore up their declining race by crossbreeding with the human species. Then there are the physical marks left behind on abductees. Hopkins shared cases with scoop marks, scars, cuts and irritations to the skins of many abductees. These marks could be found after a reported abduction on the mouth, ears, nose and genital areas. Abductees also have reported strange bruising and in some cases having implants put into their bodies.

Budd Hopkins with abductee

Hopkins speaking at MUFON event

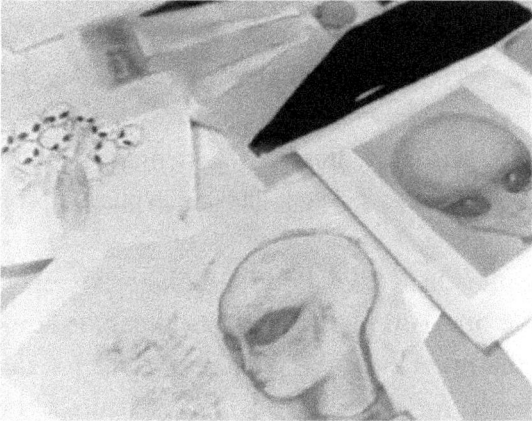

The desk of Budd Hopkins

Hopkins encouraged abductees to discuss their experiences and come together; he held free monthly group therapy sessions. The attendees at these group events were made up of people from all walks of life. At any given session you could find teachers, police officers, pilots, doctors, nurses and many other very normal occupations. These meetings gave the experiencers an opportunity to know that they were not alone and there were "other people like them," and to form a support group for one another.

Hopkins was a trained artist and not a psychotherapist or social worker. He did, however, have a gift for working with people and comparing their extraordinary claims. He compared their experiences and post lives after the abduction to PTSD (post-traumatic stress disorder) and that of individuals who experience great trauma. These intrusive and painful examinations have at times left not only physical screams but mental ones as well.

He used hypnosis to assist the experiencers to remember their clouded encounters with the "visitors." Abduction memories, according to Hopkins, rarely emerged unaided and may, at first, present to the abductees as "vague anxieties, specific phobias, bad dreams, fragmentary and disturbing memories, or what seemed like an explicable episode of missing time."

It's individuals like Budd Hopkins whom I greatly admire for not only advancing the field and dedicating their lives to the research of the phenomena but for the service they provide for the people who experienced abduction. Individuals who put their livelihood on the line for something they truly believe in and go public with their research. In his life Hopkins worked with hundreds of abductees and reassured them that they were not alone. He went on to create the Intruders Foundation in 1989, a nonprofit organization with four specific goals.

- To provide sympathetic help, understanding and personal investigation for those reporting UFO abduction experiences.

- To carry out systematic research into the abduction phenomenon through a careful study of its patterns and resulting physical traces.
- To mount an extensive program of public education.
- To develop a cadre of trained professionals in various fields to carry out all of these projects.

Budd Hopkins will always be, in my opinion, one of the pioneers of abduction research. His books and research are still being read and discussed today. It's up to the next generation of researchers to pick up where these pioneers left off and continue and study the phenomena. Hopkins's compassion and respect that he showed each one of the experiencers he encountered is so important to me, being a researcher myself. The number one goal of the Intruder Foundation is to provide sympathetic help and understanding to the experiencer. That to me says so much about the individual and the organization.

I knew I needed to include Budd Hopkins in this book, and I hope this might spark you to read his books if you haven't already. Just be prepared to explore the psychological, extremely physical, spiritual and at times high strangeness of the abduction experience. These accounts were experienced by people just like you and me, people with nothing financially to gain. If anything, to be ostracized by their peers and society. They stepped forward and told their stories, and it's up to us to listen.

# pine bush, new york

Pine Bush, New York, Restaurant

**PINE BUSH IS** a hamlet located in the town of Crawford, New York. The Hudson Valley has long been known as ground zero of UFO sightings, with locals reporting unidentified objects in the sky since the opening decades of the twentieth century. These sightings in the Pine Bush area have been reported by many residents and travelers to the area.

There are thousands of photos of mysterious craft in the sky over Pine Bush and stories involving extraterrestrials in the Hudson Valley. Investigators have been researching this area for decades and logging the activity. I have researched many theories as to why this area is a source of strange phenomena.

Many people have reported seeing orbs and bright lights that resemble balls of energy in the area. These bright orbs vanish without a trace in the fields at night. Some spectators even claim to feel electricity emanating from certain locations. Could this earth energy that's being emitted act like a beacon for the paranormal? We know that the activity that is happening in the area is attracting visitors near and far to the town of Crawford. It's an amazing feeling when you walk down Main Street in Pine Bush and see how all the storefronts of almost all the businesses have embraced their UFO and alien connection. The locals are happy to claim the title of New York's UFO Capital and display it proudly.

The town of Crawford hosts their annual Pine Bush UFO fair every year, which appeals to people of all ages. It's like an extraterrestrial convention that has something to offer everyone. The activities range from costume contests, vendors, lectures, music and an out-of-this-world parade. It's a celebration like no other, and people from all around the world flock to Pine Bush. Each year, event organizers welcome visitors from other countries, including Norway, Great Britain and Argentina. When I was in Pine Bush researching for this book project, I stopped at the best diner in the nearby galaxy, the Cup and Saucer, and talked with two out-of-state visitors from Texas and Georgia who were coming to visit and experience the UFO fair. I thought to myself, this town is truly a beacon for humans and extraterrestrials.

Debunkers have pointed out the proximity of Pine Bush to airports and military installations. Stewart Airforce base is only about fifteen miles away from the town of Crawford, and during the height of the 1980s wave, people associated the craft being seen with possible experimental craft that were being flown. The United States Army still maintains an ammunition storage annex in Newburgh. There are also smaller airstrips that craft could take off from into the skies over the area. These smaller airstrips could have been used by hoaxers, but their small planes were not being described by the experiencers. I personally find the wave and activity in the Hudson Valley extremely hard to debunk with how many witnesses there are. So many credible people have come forward and shared their experiences.

Shawangunk Mountains

There are rumors of covert and possibly sinister military activity in the area and even a secret military base with secret chambers under the Shawangunk Mountains and a subterranean tunnel connecting Stewart and Plattsburgh Air Force bases. Rumors have swirled that top-secret CIA mind-control programs are conducted in this area in an undisclosed location. This all seems like it could be taken out of an episode of *Stranger Things*. The town over the years has accumulated a tremendous amount of paranormal folklore.

## Museum That's Out of This World

The Pine Bush UFO and Paranormal Museum is more than just a collection of flying saucers and weird-looking spaceships. There's also a work map showing the locations of sightings of USOs, or unidentified submerged objects, in the world's oceans and rivers. There's also a re-creation of a reported Sasquatch sighting in Tivoli, complete with a recording of what appears to be a screaming Bigfoot and a reproduced room from Montgomery's Historic Patchett House, current home of the Wallkill River School of Art, but once a funeral home. The room reportedly had a ghost in the basement morgue.

Another room contained a reproduction of one of the stone chambers of Putnam County. I also really enjoyed how they told the story of the Betty and Barney Hill abduction that happened in nearby New Hampshire. It's a place that has something for everyone with a passion for the paranormal and who wants to educate themselves on the activity in the area. These exhibits help tell the story about the area and its connection to the paranormal activity that's been reported in it. The interactive displays in the museum help immerse the visitors into the phenomena and bring the reality of the 1980s wave into view. It's an absolutely amazing experience and one that should be applauded. More locations that have connections to paranormal phenomena should learn to embrace it like the town of Crawford has.

## Come Together

Marc D'antonio, chief photo/video analyst for MUFON and guest on many documentaries, including *Alien Invasion: Hudson Valley*, had this to say about the activity happening in the Hudson Valley. Listening to an amazing interview with D'antonio on the *Radio Forrest* podcast, he shared with listeners his view on the activity. The Hudson Valley is a place where people have been having amazing experiences for over a hundred years; there have been thousands of cases there. This place ranks as a UFO hot spot for the world.

The Hudson Valley, from a scientific perspective and using his geology background and stuff he has learned after getting his degree in astronomy, he wanted to actually decipher what is actually happening there, looking into the magnetic field or the gravitational field because both of these things vary all over the planet. Could it be a change in the rock strata, which, of course, varies all over the planet? In the Hudson Valley, the geology is quite ordinary. There are not many major concentrations; there is, however, a lot of shale, a rock that is basically made from mud forming layers over the years and basically becoming a rock over time. He goes on to talk about the gravitational field and the magnetic field in the area and using serious scientific equipment to find out what's going on there.

While filming the Discover Plus show *Alien Invasion: Hudson Valley*, they had a town hall meeting with experiencers in the hamlet of Pine Bush. D'antonio mentioned in the interview that so many people were reluctant to talk about their experiences. Some of the individuals did not want to talk; in fact, some of them did not even share the stories with each other. There was one person who started the conversation off, and he was very well known in the town. He started to share an experience that happened to him; you could see the telling of the story made him very nervous and unsettled, probably not knowing how his story would be received. What he got in return at the end of telling his story was the person next to him sharing that almost the same thing had happened to them. It was then that a floodgate opened, and many people stepped forward and shared their stories.

This small town of close-knit people who know one another started to come together and reveal personal stories of their experiences. None of them thought that they all shared these strange experiences till after that night. There were individuals who claimed that they were having abduction experiences, being taken from their beds at night, and having their home invaded by otherworldly beings. These people feel terrified and terrorized by these events. There was one person they talked with who never really wanted to come out of her house; she felt that her home was the only safe haven for her. She claimed that these beings are all over her property.

You could have a skeptical view of what's happening and think that these people are all just nuts, but when you hear stories from twenty people, fifty people and a hundred people, you have to ask yourself, are all these people nuts? D'antonio said with excitement in his voice, "No, they are not all nuts." It's very likely that this provided evidence that something really big is happening in this area of the Hudson Valley. It has been for a very long time.

I thoroughly enjoyed the interview with Marc when he brought up the town hall meeting and how so many experiencers from the town all came together and supported one another and shared their stories; that night they let one another know they are not alone. That coming together and, instead of being a singular voice, forming a community of voices is stronger and supportive for one another. Some of these stories were carried by these individuals for years for fear of being ridiculed by their friends and neighbors, but once they found out that their friends and neighbors have had the same experiences they did, they could let out a sigh and know they are not alone and can share these stories without being ridiculed and called crazy.

It's very important to have these kinds of gatherings with experiencers; it's in the sharing of their stories and information that we could truly catalog and learn about these encounters. We can help individuals heal and accept what is happening and ultimately give them a voice that can be heard.

Founded in 1993, the United Friends Observer Society support group has held regular meetings for over twenty years. As explained by the *Wallkill Valley Times*, members gather to share their stories, discuss sightings, and provide comfort to those traumatized by their run-ins with the unknown. A safe space for witnesses, contactees, abductees, and others who have had inexplicable encounters. It's a supportive and nurturing environment; the United Friends Observer Society offers UFO and paranormal enthusiasts a forum free from the skeptical eyes and snarky comments of doubters.

Richard Moschella outside the Pine Bush UFO and Paranormal Museum

Pine Bush embracing its extraterrestrial history

Pine Bush UFO and Paranormal Museum

Richard Moschella

Pine Bush UFO and Paranormal Museum

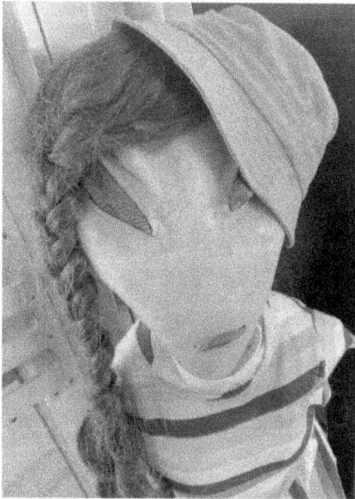

The Cup and Saucer Diner

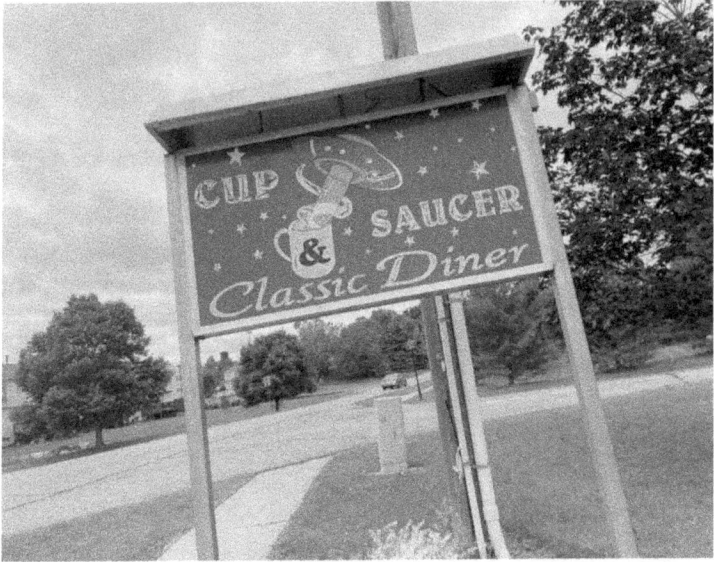

The Cup and Saucer Diner in Pine Bush, New York, fully embraces the hamlet's connection to its UFO and extraterrestrial history. The diner is decorated with items from past UFO events in the town, and its patrons are very willing to share their local stories on the area's strange paranormal events.

On a spring morning back in 2020, I sat across from an area witness who experienced multiple UFO sightings and even observed beings on the ground outside a landed craft. He described the size of the beings as about the height of young children; the encounter lasted a few moments before they returned to the craft and vanished. That was a cup of coffee I'll never forget. This man was very credible, and I could see in his eyes that this encounter left a lasting impact on him.

Richard Moschella

Outside Pine Bush UFO and Paranormal Museum

The Cup and Saucer Diner

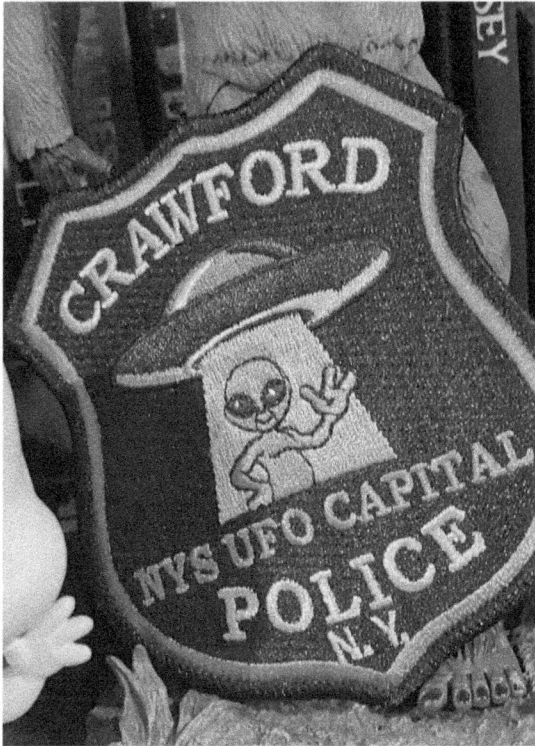

Crawford, New York, Police Patch

# darkness on the edge
# of town

**WE ARE LIVING** in a time of amazing discoveries; just look at the images that are coming in daily from the James Webb Space Telescope. We are now able to view with such great clarity distant galaxies, atmospheres and perhaps even alien planets. With the unveiling of the telescope's first images, astronomers are overjoyed with the possible discoveries that can be made now. One astronomer said it's like Christmas, Hanukkah, anniversary, graduation and Thanksgiving all rolled into one, while talking about the excitement the images have caused. As we look into the darkness on the edge of town, we might just be surprised by what we may find looking back at us.

In recent years mainstream news shows are reporting on UFO sightings; even Congress is having conversations on what they now call unexplained aerial phenomena (UAP). In the United States military, a report from 2021 stated that no evidence of aliens had been found; they could not explain some of the sightings. Their sightings were witnessed by military personnel and reported by pilots and even captured on video. The report went on to state that none of the objects had attempted to communicate with the US aviators, and no attempt had been made to communicate with them. It appears that the craft are unmanned. Many pilots avoid making reports for fear of being laughed at and having their credibility come into question.

The first public hearing on UFOs in more than fifty years included testimony from Ronald S. Moultrie, the Pentagon's top intelligence official. He noted the competing needs for transparency and secrecy in the hearing. Moultrie noted that he's a science fiction fan and that simple human curiosity means that "we want to know what's out there just like you want to know what's out there." He did add that his top goal is to keep US military personnel and bases safe.

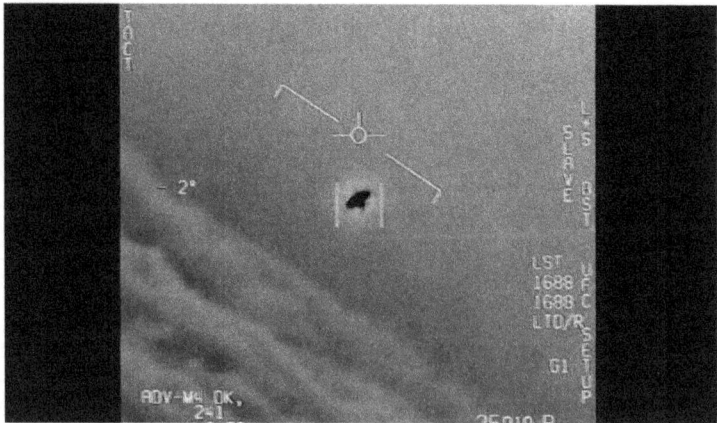

In this image from a 2015 video provided by the Department of Defense, an unexplained object is seen as it is tracked soaring high along the clouds, traveling against the wind. *Department of Defense via AP*

Moultrie also stated, "We are also mindful of our obligation to protect sensitive sources and methods." Then he went on to say, "Our goal is to strike that delicate balance, one that will enable us to maintain the public's trust while preserving those capabilities that are vital to the support of our service personnel. When looking at the government's response to UFOs and extraterrestrials in the last hundred years, is it too late to gain the public's trust? So many watershed cases involving UFOs and extraterrestrials have been discredited and swept under the rug of secrecy. I personally feel that we have gotten to a point with handheld technology that's available to the public everywhere. From powerful cell phone cameras to everything you can imagine recording video and then sharing on social media outlets. The government is scrambling to improve its image of their stance towards this phenomenon. Just think how UFO history could have been so much different if the crash at Roswell, New Mexico, happened today. Citizens armed with smartphones and sharing videos on YouTube and Tik Tok, disclosure would have been forced to take place. Again in my personal opinion, I feel that it's too little, too late. The past has already been written; it's vital to move into an era of full disclosure."

Naval Air Systems Command: Image of a UAP, seen through night-vision goggles, shown to US lawmakers

## It's Wake-Up Time

"What is true, and I'm actually being serious here, is that there is footage and records of objects in the skies that we don't know exactly what they are." –Former president Barack Obama told late-night TV host James Corden.

The time is getting close when we will know on a government level that extraterrestrials are indeed visiting Earth. I believe that they are already here. Whatever you choose to call them, the visitors, ETs, aliens or the beings, they have always been here. I feel that we have a deeper connection to them than we know. They have an interest in us, and that can be seen in the countless reports of UFO sightings and alien abductions. Is their interest in the human race more of that of a parent's observation of their children, or is it along the lines of a science project? Since the dawn of civilization, these star beings are documented to have visited the human race and have imparted knowledge and impacted ancient cultures.

We are experiencing an awakening of consciousness; planetary changes are taking place everywhere; it's coming at a time of such social discourse on a global level. We might need these visitors more than they need us at this moment in time. As Strieber stated, these visitors seek communion with us; are we ready to have that conversation? In the summer of 2022, NASA announced that it's also joining the hunt for UFOs; they are forming a team that would examine "observations of events that cannot be identified as aircraft or known natural phenomena." The space agency will bring a scientific perspective to efforts already underway by the Pentagon and intelligence agencies to help make sense of dozens of UFO sightings.

In the coming years I think we will see in our lifetime the acknowledgment on a global scale of UFOs and extraterrestrials visiting Earth. When we stand together, we are one big voice that can't be silenced.

# the paranormal hudson valley

AS A PARANORMAL INVESTIGATOR AND INTUITIVE, I have considered the Hudson Valley to be one of those thin places on the earth, where the spiritual veil is at its thinnest. The original ghost hunter, Hans Holzer, had great interest in cases in the Hudson Valley and especially in Rockland County, New York. Holzer, like myself, had a great interest in many aspects of the paranormal, including UFOs and extraterrestrials. His book *The Ufonauts*, originally published in 1979, presented overwhelming evidence for the fact that extraterrestrials are studying our life forms and taking specimens of plants and animals. This has been echoed in many reports by witnesses seeing UFO and extraterrestrial activity around water and animals, and abduction experiencers.

Another place that reports are coming from is Tuxedo Park, New York. The area that is having activity is around Lake Welch; a witness reported seeing extraterrestrials cloaking themselves in the woods around bodies of water. He has also captured multiple craft on camera.

I have talked to many people living in the town of Ramapo, and it has a very rich history of paranormal encounters. The town was established in the year of 1791, shortly after the founding of the country. The name Ramapo is derived from an Algonquin word that meant "round pond" or "sweet water." Ramapo developed on the early stagecoach route between New York City and Albany, which passed through the Ramapo pass. This area has always had interesting stories come out of it, since settlers moved into its forests.

Strange ghost lights have been reported floating in the forests, ghostly apparitions, strange creatures and lights in the sky. Just like Pine Bush, this is another area of the Hudson Valley that is full of energy. Some investigators believe in a vortex in the Ramapo Mountains where strange light anomalies have been captured coming and going. The exact spot has not been revealed but is believed to be the area around Wanaque Reservoir. This is the area that back in January 1966 something otherworldly is believed to have crashed into the reservoir. At around 6:30 in the evening, the winter sun slowly sank behind the mountains. Wanaque patrolman Joseph Cisco was sitting in his cruiser when a call came over the radio from dispatch.

It was a report of a "glowing light, possibly a fire." Then as if right out of a sci-fi movie, Cisco heard the words: "People in Oakland, Ringwood, Paterson, Totowa, and Butler claim there's a flying saucer over the Wanaque." When recalling the incident, Cisco said that he pulled into a sandpit to get his bearings, and that's when he noticed a light that looked bigger than any star. It was about the size of a softball or volleyball. It began to pulsate a white and red light. It emitted no noise and just seemed to hover in the night sky. The incident was experienced by multiple people and police offices, again highly trained and extremely credible. The craft was seen near the dam and burned a hole in the ice that covered the water. Physical evidence was left behind and one heck of a documented encounter that spanned many close-by towns.

"Something's burning a hole in the ice! Something with a bright light on it! It's going up and down!" were among the descriptions called in to police that night. When Cisco arrived, he also saw the light hovering above the water before it darted away and has never been forgotten since.

Photo of the supposed UFO over
Wanaque/NorthJersey.com

THE HUDSON VALLEY has a way of bewitching you, Washington Irving wrote in *The Legend of Sleepy Hollow*. *Some say that the place was bewitched by a High German doctor, during the early days of the settlement; others, that an old Indian chief, the prophet or wizard of his tribe, held his powwows there before the country was discovered by Master Hendrick Hudson. Certain it is, the place still continues under the sway of some witching power, that holds a spell over the minds of the good people, causing them to walk in a continual reverie. They are given to all kinds of marvelous beliefs, are subject to trances and visions, and frequently see strange sights, and hear music and voices in the air. The whole neighborhood abounds with local tales, haunted spots, and twilight superstitions; stars shoot and meteors glare oftener across the valley than in any other part of the country, and the nightmare, with her whole ninefold, seems to make it the favorite scene of her gambols.*

The Hudson Valley has always been a place where unexplainable events throughout history have occurred. From deep in its forests to its skies, it beckons visitors from this world and beyond. From personal cases that I have investigated in the Hudson Valley, I can tell you without a doubt that it's a very powerful area, and it seems that everyone who resides here in its valley has a paranormal story to tell.

Ironworks Trail, Sterling Forest, New York

# acknowledgments

A very special thank you to everyone who took the time and chatted with me about your experiences in the Hudson Valley. All the researchers and investigators who never give up the search. When we all stand together, our voices can be very powerful and heard. Thank you to Liz Holste for the countless articles you have provided. With the deepest gratitude for you, the reader, who has supported me and shares my belief that the Truth Is Out There.

Tuxedo Park, New York

# about the author

Richard Moschella lives in Rockaway, New Jersey with his wife and two children. He is the team lead and founder of the New Jersey Paranormal Project. He has investigated and researched the paranormal for many years and provides lectures and seminars on paranormal topics. He is the author of three books on spirit communication and paranormal investigating. His YouTube channel features many of the locations his team NJPP investigates.

facebook.com/richard.moschella

twitter.com/RichMoschella22

instagram.com/richiemoschella

# also by richard moschella

My New Jersey Paranormal

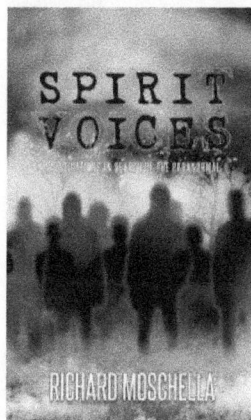

Spirit Voices: Investigations in Search of the
Paranormal

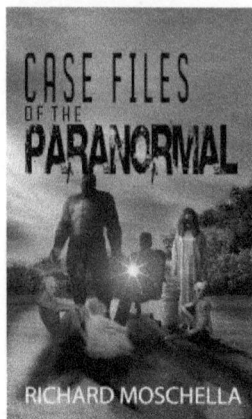

Case Files of the Paranormal

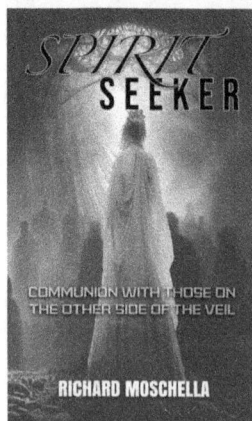

Spirit Seeker

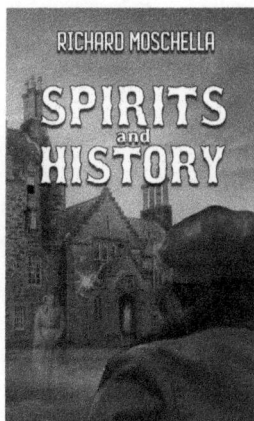

Spirits and History

www.ingramcontent.com/pod-product-compliance
Lightning Source LLC
Chambersburg PA
CBHW022335280326
41934CB00006B/644